I PROTEST

I PROTEST

By G. Bromley Oxnam

Harper & Brothers Publishers
New York

48894

SX 33
Qx 5i

I PROTEST

Library of Congress catalogue card number: 54-6899

PREFACE

THE INFORMER is infiltrating American life at the national, state and local level. He invades the privacy of the home, reports on classroom discussion and library accessions, and summons his colleagues to challenge the sanctity of the church. He is a man of the shadows, born of fear and contributing to it. He speaks in whispers. Justice William O. Douglas describes him as "nameless and faceless." He is not subpoenaed, answers no roll call, dares not face the man he accuses. He is as un-American as the Nazi Gauleiter or the Russian commissar. But he is here. He strikes at the heart of American freedom. He is a creature of the police state, an alien and malignant growth. Those who employ him or sustain him insist there is no fear upon the American campus; no fear in the government service; no fear in the motion picture, the television or radio industry; no fear in the church; in fact no fear at all except as it is conjured up by the liberals, who are alleged to be unaware of the Communist threat to freedom.

This denial of the presence of fear is as false as the presence of fear is a fact. The whisper has entered American life for the first time. A people unafraid, heretofore ready to speak its mind boldly, a proud people is becoming a silent people. The American is holding his tongue. If this were due to more serious thought, it would be well. But it is due to fear. Communism can never be answered by fearful people who stand silent. And strangely enough this fear results in large measure from the un-American activities of elected representatives of the American people who have been charged with "investigating" subversive activities. It arises from the activities of wide-ranging private agencies, vigilante in spirit, of mixed motives, but pursuing methods of the police state that run the gamut from wire-tapping to the maintenance of the dossier.

Industrialists, who stupidly subsidized Hitler and secretly assumed that he was "their" man, were the first to learn that free enterprise dies at the hand of the dictator, and the sophisticated who laughed and called Hitler a buffoon were among the first to behold him as the beast and to be shut up in Buchenwald. The reactionary coalition of isolationists, purblind industrialists and alien-minded prelates may profit by the lessons of Hitler Germany. Whether this coalition is capable of learning is yet to be decided, but there can be no doubt among those who would preserve our freedom that to appease such tendencies will bring the train of tyranny that appeasement brings whenever we compromise with the tyrant mind, right or left. The threat must be met head on, wisely, fearlessly, successfully.

There is a rightful and necessary place for Congressional investigation. It is necessary for Congress to investigate in order that it may have information upon which to base sound legislation. It may be necessary to investigate the agencies chartered by the Congress to be certain that the terms of reference are carried out faithfully and in the interests of the common good. Investigation has at times resulted in information of great value to the nation. It has an educational value, and in some cases the exposure made by investigators has been significant. It is not the propriety of Congressional investigation that is the concern of this book.

The Communist Party is a conspiracy. Conspirators ought to be discovered, tried in due process and, if found guilty, punished. That is taken for granted.

This book is concerned with procedures that repudiate American tradition and practice, procedures that involve the informer, that riddle our life with distrust, that set American against American, that tend to label sound reform as subversive, that make no distinction between progress and revolution, procedures carried on by staffs too largely composed of ex-Communists and often incompetent, or by politicians some of whom appear prone to capitalize upon hysteria for political advantage.

The American must protest. He must do more. He must throttle this threat to freedom. He must preserve the free society.

I PROTEST

I T WAS a sultry day in mid-summer. Earlier in the morning, the
flags in front of the Supreme Court Building billowed out in
pride, but now, with breezes gone, hung listlessly. A year before, I
had been appointed to serve in Washington and with no little pride
took up residence in the Methodist Building which is superbly located
on Maryland Avenue across the street from the Capitol grounds and
directly opposite the Supreme Court Building. Soon after our arrival,
I heard a call at dawn.

"Come quickly," Mrs. Oxnam said. She was standing by one of the
windows overlooking the Supreme Court Plaza. "Look, they are
raising the flags." The beautiful banners were pulled to their places
atop the heavy flagpoles that stood secure in bronze-sculptured bases.
"Now I know what it means," she said quietly.

"What does what mean?" I queried.

" 'By the dawn's early light,' " she replied.

There was no breeze at one-thirty on Tuesday afternoon, July 21,
1953, as we walked from the Methodist Headquarters to the Old
House of Representatives' Office Building. Wisely, or unwisely, I had
demanded a hearing before the Committee on Un-American Activities of the House of Representatives. And now I was in for it.

For seven years that Committee had released so-called "files" containing false material concerning me. These releases appeared upon
official letterheads of the Committee, and were signed by an official
clerk. Later, in response to my insistent inquiries, the chairman of the
Committee declared that the Committee did not vouch for the accuracy of the material released, and that such releases did not repre-

sent a conclusion or an opinion of the Committee. The releases carried no such disclaimer, in my case. Repeated requests for correction of the files were ignored. I had been informed that the proper way to get this unevaluated and unverified material eliminated from the files was to appear in person before the Committee and to make a formal demand for the ending of this vicious practice. Congressman John S. Wood, the former chairman of the Committee, and Congressman Harold H. Velde, its present chairman, had both pointed out that the proper way to clear such a matter was to request a hearing. Congressman Donald L. Jackson had said, "Anyone who feels that he has come under public disapprobation" or has run "afoul of the Committee on Un-American Activities . . . has redress before the greatest forum . . . in the entire world, the forum of the Congress of the United States, in order to answer any allegations, in order to meet any charges which he himself feels are not founded in fact." When, with considerable reluctance, I had requested such a hearing, Congressman Gordon H. Scherer, in an open letter to the Cincinnati *Enquirer* after the hearing, said, "It was one which was demanded by the Bishop and to which I was personally opposed because I knew that the Bishop's demand for this hearing was for the purpose of obtaining a forum to attack us, and not, as he claimed, to correct alleged misinformation about him in the file."

This untruthful statement as to my motives made by Congressman Scherer after the hearing is typical of similar statements made by other members of the Committee. Congressman Jackson, on the floor of the House, had accused me of "serving God on Sunday and the Communist front for the balance of the week." Mr. Scherer knew that religious bodies across the nation had passed resolutions condemning Mr. Jackson and demanding he apologize publicly. The Baltimore Conference of the Methodist Church had unanimously demanded such an apology "for his disrespectful remarks to our distinguished bishop and the affront given the Methodist Church." Mr. Jackson's reply simulated dignity. He said, "The case of Bishop Oxnam cannot be settled by resolutions or by public releases. Certain facts and allegations can only be answered before a duly constituted body which has the authority to take testimony under oath. Inasmuch as the material to which Bishop Oxnam objects is in the possession of the House Committee on Un-American Activities, it would appear that this committee is the proper forum before which the matter should be heard. If the material relevant to Bishop Oxnam's alleged activities in and on behalf of Communist front organizations is without foundation, it would appear desirable for all concerned for the Bishop to appear publicly for the purpose of setting the record straight."

Mr. Scherer knew this statement had been issued. He knew the Committee refused to vouch for the accuracy of the file it released. He knew no "investigator" had ever called upon me to so much as make inquiry. He knew Mr. Velde had publicly stated he had issued a standing invitation to appear before the Committee. Newspapermen had told me that some Committee members had said I was afraid to appear. What else could a self-respecting citizen do than to demand a hearing? It appears never to have entered the heads of these gentlemen that they should have come to me with at least an inquiry, not to say apology. They had released the false and damaging allegations, and when informed, had done nothing to rectify the files or to redress the wrong.

Friends, in whose judgment I had confidence, urged me to "call their bluff" and to demand a hearing. Others, equally wise, said, "Do not dignify them by such a request. You will be admitting the right of the state to catechize the church. Your presence may open the door to further inroads upon the principle of the separation of state and church." An experienced newscaster said, "Don't be naïve, Bishop. These men do not want the truth. They are out to destroy you. You have dared to criticize them. You are not dealing with the integrity that characterizes the classroom or the church. This is political rough and tumble. No holds will be barred." I had weighed the conflicting advice, and finally sent a telegram on June 5, 1953, to Congressman Harold H. Velde:

RESPECTFULLY REQUEST OPPORTUNITY TO BE HEARD BY YOUR COMMITTEE TO ANSWER FALSE ALLEGATIONS REGARDING ME APPEARING IN YOUR FILES AND RELEASED BY YOUR COMMITTEE. PLEASE ADVISE WHEN I MAY BE HEARD.

The classic Corinthian columns of the Supreme Court Building were full of light, and it was not easy to read the great-lettered inscription beneath the pediment, "EQUAL JUSTICE UNDER LAW." The trees surrounding the Capitol were at the height of their beauty, rich in summer's green. As I looked toward the Capitol dome, I thought of the service of a few months before when I had pulled the cords unveiling the statue of Jason Lee, a Methodist missionary who had pioneered the West and had been chiefly responsible for bringing Oregon into the Union and who now was to take his place in Statuary Hall among the immortals. Vice-President Richard M. Nixon had been present, and I recalled that he had been a member of the Committee I was so soon to face. I thought, too, of the inauguration in January. I had sat in the President's Section, and had been deeply moved by the modesty of the man, by the simple prayer he read, and by the fact that his first act after becoming President was to kiss Mrs. Eisenhower. I would have ridiculed the suggestion, had it been made, that within a few hours the chairman of the Committee on Un-American Activities would try to keep me from quoting a statement made by the General in 1945.

I knew there were members of the Committee who were more interested in saving face than in facing facts; but I was determined to treat them with the respect due elected representatives of the people, even though I had read the disgraceful record of Committee hearings under J. Parnell Thomas, its former chairman, and had noted the rantings of John Elliott Rankin, one of its former members. Newspapermen had reported the remarks of Congressmen Clardy, Jackson and Velde, and friends had reported conversation with Mr. Scherer. Others had said, "Be on your guard. This is not investigation. It is intimidation. This is a twentieth-century Inquisition."

Charles C. Parlin, head of one of the great law firms of New York City and a distinguished layman of our church, Mrs. Oxnam, and I walked to the offices of Robert L. Kunzig, recently appointed counsel for the Committee. Mr. Kunzig had suggested that we come there so that he might escort us to the Caucus Room where the hearing was to be held. He told us the hearing room had been full since noon, and that long lines now extended down the marble staircase and into the street. We went upstairs. Mr. Kunzig was about to lead us into the room through the door used by Committee members. Someone rushed up and whispered to him. I heard the words "Jackson" and "clergymen." Mr. Kunzig said we would have to enter by the main door. So we went down the hall.

It was true. The hall was filled with people seeking admittance. There was a column, several abreast, from the entrance door down the staircase as far as I could see. Friends greeted us. Dr. John Q. Schisler, one of the most influential educators of Methodism and executive secretary of the Division of the Local Church of our General Board of Education, left his place in the line and said, "Bishop, we may not get in, but we want you to know we are with you." Officers opened up a way, and we pushed through to three seats that had been held for us.

I learned later that the reason we could not be admitted by way of the Committee anteroom was that Mr. Jackson, duped by a little group of clergymen representing some small fundamentalist splinter sects, led in some cases by men who had been deposed from the ministry by the great denominations, had invited these gentlemen to be present as his guests. He had reserved the front row on the left for them. They had "channeled," to use their own word, information to Mr. Jackson, and he had fallen for it. An "investigator" worthy of the name would have ascertained the difference between this little group of dissidents who call themselves the American Council of Christian Churches and the National Council of the Churches of Christ in the United States of America. The National Council is not a church, but is the churches themselves in co-operation at the national level. This great co-operative agency of thirty denominations and representing thirty-five million members might have helped Mr. Jackson get the truth; but he proved gullible and was misled by others. He had appeared at a "mammoth mass meeting" in Constitution Hall some time before and had received a petition carrying "a hundred thousand signatures." Actually, there were about six hundred persons at the meeting. Did he know how the signatures had been obtained? In Nashville, a booth on a down-town street had carried large placards reading, "SIGN THE PETITION. BACK THE COMMITTEE ON UN-AMERICAN ACTIVITIES. HELP INVESTIGATE COMMUNISTS IN RELIGION." Another smaller card read, "LET THE BLOOD OF JESUS BE THE ONLY RED IN YOUR CHURCH." A lady in the booth, speaking into a microphone, called upon the people to sign.

A man charged with the responsibilities of a Congressman might have asked these people, "Whom do you represent? What churches are in your Council? Have you an audited statement of your financial transactions?"

Perhaps he heard the broadcast from Los Angeles in which the Reverend Claude Bunsel said, "For several years the American Council of Christian Churches has been channeling information about Communist and pro-Communist clergymen to the House Committee on Un-American Activities and urging that an investigation be made."

Mr. Jackson's "guests" were in the front row. They were apparently in for the "kill." Is there any hatred more damaging to the soul than that of one who claims to speak for a God of love but who, because of inner frustrations and unrealized ambitions, lives in a constant inferiority complex, seeking the publicity satisfactions of attacking others, searing his soul with envy, and coming at last to the place where he repudiates Christ's command, and in desperation cries out, "Thou shalt hate thy neighbor as thyself"? The publications and preaching of this little group are filled with venom. Most hatred for others begins as self-hatred. There is nothing to do but to forgive such persons. None the less, there is an obligation to explain them and to expose them.

Many friends were in the hearing room, among them Dr. Samuel McCrae Cavert, the general secretary of the National Council of Churches, who has done more than any one person to build the structure of interdenominational co-operation in America. He had come down from New York. A wiser man than Mr. Jackson might have noted the names of great laymen associated with Dr. Cavert in the National Council, among them, Harvey S. Firestone, Jr., chairman of the Firestone Tire and Rubber Company; Harry A. Bullis, chairman of the board, General Mills, Inc.; Dr. Walter C. Coffey, president emeritus, University of Minnesota; Hugh M. Comer, president, Avondale Mills; John Holmes, president of Swift and Company; Charles R. Hook, chairman of the Armco Steel Corporation; B. E. Hutchinson, chairman of the Finance Committee of the Chrysler Corporation; the Honorable Walter H. Judd, a member of the present Congress; Admiral Ben Morrell, president and chairman of the board of the Jones and Laughlin Steel Corporation; John Nuveen, investment broker; Edward L. Ryerson, chairman of the board, the Inland Steel Company; Noel Sargent, secretary of the National Association of Manufacturers; Morris B. Shiskin, economist with the American Federation of Labor; Harold E. Stassen, former Governor of Minnesota and at present a prominent member of the Eisenhower administration; Charles P. Taft, lawyer; Charles E. Wilson, former president of the General Electric Company; and Robert E. Wilson, chairman of the Standard Oil Company of Indiana. But Congressman Jackson, an "investigator," had failed to make inquiry concerning the supporters of his "informers."

Francis S. Harmon who, with Eric Johnston, led the Motion Picture Producers Association and who, as a distinguished layman, is serving the National Council so conspicuously in its Budget and Business Administration, as well as in Riverside Church in New York City, a man who had had long experience with this Committee when it so viciously attacked the motion-picture industry, was present. I was told that a hundred Congressmen had requested seats. Elmer Rogers, a distinguished Masonic leader, came forward to greet me, and said that Thomas J. Harkins, Sovereign Grand Commander of the Supreme Council of Thirty-third Degree Masons of the Southern Jurisdiction, was there.

Sitting there on the front row, I wondered. There was the roar of conversation. Before me was the bench soon to be occupied by nine members of the Committee. On the right, the seats were filled, I was told, by Congressmen. On the left, were batteries of television and motion-picture cameras, sound-recording devices, brilliant lights flashing on and off, the words "Testing, Testing" heard above the din. Every square foot between the front row and the Committee bench was crowded by journalists. I saw some whose names are household words. After all, had it been wise to subject myself to all this? I knew the Committee, or at least some of its members, were playing for keeps. I had thought the proper answer to the Committee practice of releasing unverified and unevaluated material was personal protest or silence. It is not too difficult to take misrepresentation individually, but when the misrepresentation questioned the loyalty of the Protestant churches of the nation, silence seemed no longer the answer, and no matter how much one might abhor public appearance, it seemed necessary to risk it.

Was the attack on the Protestant clergy prelude to something even more sinister? Who were really back of the attack? What was their objective? It was strange that the attack had centered upon Protestant leaders who had been most active in developing Protestant unity. Before the day had passed, I had come to the conclusion that churchmen must speak out everywhere, and educators too. This was too much like the pre-Hitler atmosphere, too much like the practice of Stalin's commissars. There was an underlying assumption akin to the basic assumption of totalitarianism, namely, that the state has the right to determine the philosophy to which everyone who lives within the state must give assent. The totalitarian holds that the state has the right and duty to mobilize every impact upon the mind to the end that the citizen shall be coerced into accepting the predetermined philosophy. These men, charged with investigating un-American activities, had presumed to set themselves up to define Americanism. I knew that totalitarians hold that deviation is disloyalty; that dissent is treason.

Later, when I read the August, 1953, *Atlantic Monthly* article by Mr. Abe Fortas entitled "Outside the Law," it seemed to me he was describing precisely my reaction to the experiences of that day. He wrote,

The purpose of the proceeding is not to determine whether the accused did something, or even whether he has had, uttered, or been associated with "subversive" ideas. Rather, it is whether on the basis of his entire life he does or does not meet the tribunal's conceptions of freedom from disloyalty. In substance, the burden of establishing virtue or conformity is on the accused.

Referring to some but not all of these inquisitors, he says,

The hearing has become a weapon of persecution, a useful tool to the demagogue, a device for the glory of the prosecutor, and a snare for the accused.

The next day, the Committee on motion of Congressman Clyde Doyle having voted "that this Committee has no record of any Communist Party affiliation or membership by Bishop Oxnam," Congressman Morgan M. Moulder of Missouri said, "After hearing and careful consideration of all the evidence, it is my opinion that Bishop Oxnam is not and never has been a Communist or a Communist sympathizer. On the contrary, he convinced me that he has vigorously opposed Communism, and has fought hard against the philosophy and conditions which breed Communism. However, I do believe Bishop Oxnam to be a liberal, but not more so than Thomas Jefferson or Theodore Roosevelt. It is my opinion that he is a loyal American citizen and is intensely possessed with the spirit of God and the work of the church he serves."

Mr. Jackson demurred, "My vote had nothing to do with 'clearing' or finding guilt, neither of which finding is within the jurisdiction of the Committee as constituted." This was in response to the nation-wide press reaction to Congressman Doyle's motion, which Mr. Jackson himself had seconded. The press generally accepted the statement that Mr. Doyle himself subsequently made, "I consider it to be a clearance of the Bishop of any charges or inferences that he was affiliated with the Communist Party. Not one scintilla of evidence was presented to show that he was a Communist or willingly or knowingly a member of any Communist front."

In less than two months, Congressman Jackson who had rushed to the House floor to explain that his seconding of Congressman Doyle's motion had nothing to do with clearing or finding guilt, "neither of which finding is within the jurisdiction of the Committee as consti-tuted," became party to just such a "clearing." Miss Lucille Ball, to quote Mr. Jackson's phrase, had "run afoul of the House Com-mittee on Un-American Activities." The Minneapolis *Star* for Sep-tember 14, 1953, in a lead editorial entitled "Lucy versus the Bishop," said,

Certainly it was gallant of Representative D. L. Jackson (R. Calif.) to make a special statement for the committee giving the television-comedy star a clean bill of political health. It could so easily have gone quite differ-ently. Here was a wealthy figure in show business who had actually registered as a Communist voter (in 1936) for a reason that might have been held up to ridicule—"because Grandpa wanted us all to." . . . More-over, even though she has declared it was without her consent, she appar-

ently was, at least temporarily, designated a member of the California State
Central Committee of the Communist Party. And she signed a sponsoring
certificate on behalf of a Communist candidate for the State Assembly.

The editorial continues,

The mixed feelings with which one must regard Miss Ball's vindication
are inspired not by the expeditious handling of her case, but by the con-
trast between it and the treatment accorded other persons entangled in the
Committee's investigations. It is more than a bit depressing, for example,
to compare the alacrity with which the Committee "cleared" Miss Ball and
its inexplicable slowness to give equal clearance to Methodist Bishop
G. Bromley Oxnam.

The editorial quotes Mr. Jackson as saying, "The Committee is de-
parting from its usual procedure so that fact may be separated from
rumor and no damage done Miss Ball," and remarks,

Compare that, with Mr. Jackson's behavior after Bishop Oxnam made
his tremendously effective appearance before the Committee in July. . . .
One must wonder what there was in Lucille Ball's defense which Jackson
found so much more convincing than Bishop Oxnam's—so convincing, in
fact, as to justify the Committee's making the kind of judgment which
it was not authorized to make when the Bishop's reputation had been
maligned.

The Christian Century for September 30, 1953, treated the incident
editorially under the humorous title "The Big Bad Bishop and the
Strawberry Blonde," concluding,

Here was an admitted instance of Communist affiliation—quite a con-
trast to the unsubstantiated innuendoes in the case of Bishop Oxnam. How
did Mr. Jackson proceed? Instantly he assured the press that Miss Ball had
meant nothing by her actions and that, so far as the Un-American Activities
Committee was concerned, she was entirely in the clear! Would his treatment of Bishop Oxnam's request for an apology have been different if
(1) the Bishop had an $8 million contract from a television network, (2)
was one of Hollywood's most valuable properties, (3) lived in Southern

California, and (4) the better part of the nation was taking the evening off once a week to cry "I love Bromley!"

The physical setup a witness faces is most disconcerting. I had demanded a hearing so that the files might be corrected. Respectful letters requesting revision had proved to be fruitless. The counsel for the Committee had inquired a day or two before whether I would object to the proceedings being televised and broadcast. I said I had no objection. I had insisted upon a public hearing, because I was fearful that unless the press could be present, a Committee that had misrepresented an individual over a period of seven years might continue to do so, and the truth of the hearings might never reach the public. I never realized what it would mean to sit before bright lights all afternoon, all through the evening, and into the next morning.

I do not know whether these uncomfortable and distracting physical conditions are the result of thoughtlessness or of design, but I know some consideration ought to be given to the convenience of the witness. Mr. Parlin and I sat at a table. There were, I think, seven microphones or recording devices in front of me, so placed that it was impossible to have my papers before me in any way that gave easy access to the documents. I had files in two brief cases, and thus had to reach for a file, look for a document, put it back into the brief case. It was very difficult to handle materials under such circumstances, particularly in view of the fact that I never knew what item was coming up next. An investigating committee which is supposed to be seeking information should make it easier for a witness to present it. The bright lights necessary for television were directly behind the Committee, and therefore were shining in my eyes all the time they were on, throughout the day. It meant that when I lifted my eyes to look toward Committee members, I was almost blinded. It was extremely difficult to read from documents.

It is like playing baseball upon the home grounds of your opponent. That is a disadvantage, but in such a hearing the committee makes the rules and can change them at pleasure, and it does. I was soon to learn that a question is asked, you start to answer, you are interrupted by another Committeeman. This happened too often to be an accident.

A Congressional committee is endowed with power by Congress. A witness sits at the floor level. In front of him and above him like judges upon the bench are the members of the committee. Directly in front of me was the committee counsel with his assistant, and, in turn, another assistant. Then there are the investigators sitting there, how many I did not ascertain.

I was alone, except for counsel. If Mr. Parlin, with his brilliant legal equipment, had been able to interpose objections or to make suggestions, he could have been most helpful. But the rules of the Committee denied to the counsel the right to say a single word. He could whisper to me occasionally, if he saw fit; but that was almost impossible, I was soon to learn, because if there were the least delay in answering a question, a member of the Committee would call out peremptorily, "Witness, Witness." All that my counsel was allowed to do publicly was to state his name, his address, and the fact that he was a member of the New York Bar. In a word, an individual is alone, facing a Committee which possesses great power. He must strike a balance between answers that will convince and answers that may antagonize. Politicians granted power can become ferine when crossed.

When we were called to take our places, Mr. Velde stood. The oath was administered. I felt for a moment like an accused at a criminal trial.

I was faced by procedures designed to discredit. But the Committee reckoned without the press. Distinguished journalists and radio commentators were present. Every word was recorded; and that evening carefully edited sections were televised to the nation. People had a chance to see what was going on, and the response of the press the next day was heartening beyond description. Journalists know that a free press is essential to a free society and that procedures that jeopardize freedom, whether it be of a churchman or an educator, a businessman or a labor leader, will sooner or later mean the end of a free press and the snuffing out of freedom itself.

Who are these men who sit in judgment upon American citizens? They are, it is true, the elected representatives of the people. They are therefore entitled to respect; but are they qualified to define Americanism and to demand that their definition of Americanism shall be observed by all Americans? Is there a proper investigation of investigators that should be had? What are the real forces back of Mr. Velde? Who is back of Mr. Scherer? What have been his contributions to Americanism? What is the educational equipment Donald L. Jackson brings to his task? And who is Mr. Clardy? Without calling the roll, Americans should consider carefully this invasion of the thinking of other Americans by elected representatives. It must not be forgotten that J. Parnell Thomas was padding payrolls at the same time he was serving as chairman of the House Committee on Un-American Activities. He was subsequently tried, found guilty, and served time in the penitentiary.

Does this mean that the Committee members who sat with him are also involved and subject to such criticism? Of course not. But Committee members, in the procedures they follow, assume that association with any group later alleged to be subversive means that the individual himself was subversive.

Abe Fortas, in the article referred to, presents an illuminating illustration. He says, referring to these hearings:

The accused has no real opportunity to volunteer his own defense or explanation. He has no foreknowledge of the lines of inquiry and no access to documents that the committee may use. In notorious instances, the form and technique of questioning seem designed to confuse or entrap him, and to prevent explanation rather than to elicit it.

In fact, some aspects of the procedure used by at least one of the leading committees invite the suspicion that the marshaling of the so-called evidence is designed not to test a point but to convey a sensational and damaging impression to the press and public. One technique frequently employed by a committee is to ask the accused to identify—merely to identify—a named person. Let's call him Mr. Ting. The accused states he has read in the press that Mr. Ting is a leading Communist. Committee counsel then asks an investigator, who has been solemnly sworn, to identify a document. The document is elaborately identified, in what seems to the lawyer to be a parody of courtroom behavior. Next, it is read into the record; and it shows that Mr. Ting was engaged in some nefarious Communist activity. The committee then proceeds to question the accused about a totally different subject.

Throughout all of this drama, the accused sits bewitched, bothered, and bewildered—the focus of hundreds of eyes in the hearing room and perhaps at the television sets. He may have had no connection with Mr. Ting. He knows nothing about the incident in the exhibit. The committee does not even suggest that he was connected with it. But the accused is as definitely implicated in the minds of the audience as if he himself had committed the described act of subversion or Communism.

I want to be fair, but I am dealing here with a procedure that is really, as one of the Committee himself said, "damnable."

These Committeemen pontificate upon the basis of information received a few days before in some secret hearing. A professional witness swears that a certain man was a Communist. Without hearing the accused, without cross-examining the accuser, or checking his record for veracity, Committeemen accept the word of a former Communist. They declare the accused is a Communist, and even publish the names of the accused in the annual report of the Committee. The American principle that a man is innocent until proved guilty to the satisfaction of a jury and after facing his accusers is rejected.

Justice William O. Douglas of the Supreme Court recently spoke of the "witch-hunt and the merchants of hate." He said, "We put a cloak of anonymity over a growing underground of informers. Men are adjudged on the whispered accusations of faceless people not known to the accused . . . and the privacy of the home is increasingly invaded by wire-tappers. . . . Anxieties and suspicions are aroused, until a community does not know what to believe or whom to trust, until even old neighbors suspect one another. More and more, people conclude that the only safe thing to do is to conform: either to stand silent or to join the hunt."

Upon the secret uncorroborated and unchecked testimony of former conspirators, admittedly at one time members of the Communist party, Committeemen trained in the law repudiate their legal principles and announce, "He is a Communist."

Of course, no such statement was made concerning me. Not even a professional stool pigeon would dare to make such a ridiculous charge, but the Committee apparently hoped to justify its inexcusable practice of releasing falsehoods on official letterheads by insinuating that I had been active in "Communist fronts." It was soon to become apparent that the "investigators," obviously out to prove guilt rather than to ascertain the truth, were making no headway. They then resorted to one of the abominable practices of some Committeemen. They began to express personal opinions which so often make headlines. I was "muddled in thinking," one who was on the "sucker list," "a dupe." But I had an advantage. I knew the facts. The facts could have been secured by the Committee years before by a very simple device which apparently never occurred to the "investigators." They could have made a personal inquiry, either in writing or by sending someone over to see me. I knew, therefore, that some of the "dupes" sat on the bench, and lacked the intellectual equipment to understand the duping process.

There have been notable exceptions in these Committees, and some men have rendered the nation valuable service; but some of the men

I faced that day, trained in the law, seemed unaware of participating in procedures that to me are outside the law.

◀ ❘ ▶

I protest against the use of the House floor to defame. It is at once ungentlemanly and un-American to abuse the privilege of immunity by broadcasting a falsehood from the House of Representatives. There is no Congressional immunity from the Biblical injunction, "Thou shalt not bear false witness."

THE AMERICAN people have wisely granted immunity to their representatives when speaking in the House or the Senate, because they want these representatives to have full freedom to express their minds. But the American people never envisioned such abuse of immunity as practiced by Congressman Donald L. Jackson. Mr. Jackson is a smooth talking, superficial opportunist. After having condemned Congressman Velde's alleged intention to investigate the churches, he saw a political opportunity. He apologized for what he confesses was a misunderstanding upon his part, and rushed to the defense of the chairman of the Committee. During the course of that address he, for the first time in American history, singled out a bishop for vicious attack. Either Mr. Jackson relied upon his incompetent investigation staff and therefore spoke out upon the basis of the misinformation which incompetency produced for him, or Mr. Jackson was duped by others who placed in his hands alleged evidence which he himself never checked for accuracy.

In any case, he referred to me as "a gentleman who now presumes to criticize the work of your House Committee in its investigation of identified Communists." He appeared to assume the Committee was sacrosanct, above criticism. He had excoriated the Ford Foundation because it had appropriated fifteen million dollars to study contemporary threats to civil liberty. He then said, "Bishop Bromley has been to the Communist front what Man-O'-War was to thoroughbred horse-racing, and no one except the good Bishop pays much attention to his fulminations these days. Having served God on Sunday and the Communist front for the balance of the week over such a long period of time, it is no great wonder that the Bishop sees an investigating committee in every vestry. If re-printing Bishop Oxnam's record of aid and comfort to the Communist front would serve any useful purpose, I would ask permission to insert it here, but suffice it so say that the record is available to any Member who cares to request it from the Committee." This, of course, was so patently false as to create resentment across the nation.

Later in the hearing Mr. Jackson was to introduce information alleging that I had spoken at a radical meeting in Los Angeles, California. He had to go back to 1923 to find the so-called information. Actually, I had not addressed that meeting. Had Mr. Jackson made a serious effort to get the truth which is certainly a fundamental requirement for an investigator, he might well have gone to the corner of Sixth and Gladys Avenue. There he would have found the buildings of the Church of All Nations; the Boys' Club Building given by two prominent businessmen, Charles Brown Voorhees and Royal Robert Bush. He might have learned that before I left Los Angeles a thousand boys belonged to the Boys' Clubs of the All Nations Foundation, that the juvenile delinquency rates of the East Side of the city which had been the highest in all of Los Angeles County had been reduced until they were lower than the average for the city as a whole. He might have secured the testimony of judges and juvenile officers and churchmen. But he did not get the facts. He was interested in buttressing the charges he had enunciated upon the House floor. He would have found the Chapel a memorial to Walter Harrison Fisher. He might even have sat in that Chapel and have asked the question, Is the man who was responsible for this institution the person I have defamed? Had he looked to the altar window with its glorious glass of changing color, designed by Wilson who had once done creative work for Tiffany Studios, he would have seen the figure of the Christ seated upon a throne, his arms extended in loving invitation. I had asked Mr. Wilson to design a window in which Jesus might be revealed as King of kings and as Servant of all.

He could have stepped into the next building, the Community House, and there in the memorial to Dana W. Bartlett whose years of distinguished service had meant so much to Los Angeles, he would have found the volumes of one of the first libraries upon the East Side. He could have gone back to the Clinic Building where thirty years ago a staff of twenty-one physicians had given its time free, and literally thousands had received medical attention which otherwise would have been denied them. He might have read the bronze tablets upon the building. But he did not. On the contrary, he looked up heated newspaper columns telling of a political campaign in which, as a young minister, I had been foolish enough to run for the Board of Education. He could have interviewed distinguished educators at the University of Southern California or at the University of California at Los Angeles. He might have conferred with Chancellor Rufus Bernhard von KleinSmid from whom I had received the honorary doctorate in law. He might have journeyed to Stockton, California, to the beautiful campus of the College of the Pacific, the oldest institution of higher education in the state, and have learned that Chancellor Tully Cleon Knoles, revered by thousands of students in California, had conferred the honorary doctorate in divinity upon me. He could have talked with the Bishop of the Methodist Church and the leading ministers of the city of all denominations. He could have met scores of businessmen, had he desired, who knew me. But no, Mr. Jackson must have information to prove that someone had served a Communist front. Had he not said so?

Integrity is essential to investigation. Mr. Jackson knows that he secured information that was not in the files at the time I had requested a hearing, and sought to introduce it during the hearing. The purpose of the hearing was the revision of the files. He even admitted that some of the material had come in too late—material which he himself had "developed," to use his word—for photostating. Some of the Committee members did not have the material before them during the hearing.

No doubt Mr. Jackson's trips to the coast were at public expense. Did he ascertain from anyone what I had taught at the University of Southern California relative to communism? Such class notes might have set his mind at rest. No, the objective was to defend a position he had taken. How much simpler for a man to admit that he had been misinformed and apologize for having borne false witness. But Mr. Donald L. Jackson seemed to be carrying a personal grudge. No doubt it grew out of the embarrassment he faced the day we engaged in debate on the American Forum of the Air.

The hearing began with all members of the Committee present. The record indicates that Robert L. Kunzig, Counsel; Frank S. Tavenner, Jr., Counsel; Louis J. Russell, Chief Investigator; Raphael I. Nixon, Director of Research; and Mrs. Juliette Joray, Acting Clerk, were present. Thus an individual who had requested revision of files was confronted by nine Congressmen, five members of the staff, and I believe others. Mr. Clardy, much given to talking off the cuff, is reported to have said that the secret hearings in New York were preliminary to my hearing. In a word, careful preparation had been made. It was clear before many minutes had passed that the purpose was less that of correcting the files than of discrediting a witness who had dared to criticize individuals who regard themselves as above criticism.

Mr. Velde called the Committee to order, and in a brief statement announced, "Bishop Oxnam is here at his own request, and in keeping with an established policy of the Committee to grant a hearing to any citizen who asserts that he has been in any way adversely affected by virtue of any action taken by the Committee." He added, "This is a fundamental right attached to American citizenship, and the Committee welcomes such opportunity." He stated that I had informed the Committee that information in the files was in error and that I had been harmed. He added, "To the end that the facts of the allegations may be determined, the Committee extended an invitation to Bishop Oxnam to appear, which invitation was accepted." Having felt the reaction to his original announcement widely interpreted as investigating in the field of religion, he particularly insisted that this hearing "should not be interpreted by anyone as an investigation initiated by the Congress into the field of religion." Mr. Velde tried to disassociate the statements made by individual members of the Committee from actions of the Committee itself. Had Mr. Velde been a little more careful along this line himself both before and after the hearing, his warning would have been more impressive.

Investigating committees set up their own procedures. Irresponsible chairmen mean irresponsible procedures. A committee of one Congress may reject the procedures of a former Congress. It becomes the rule of men rather than the rule of law.

I had insisted upon an opening statement. How could any individual coming to a committee and demanding redress do other than to present the matters to the committee that he desired discussed? There was strenuous objection to an initial statement upon my part; and I was informed that the Committee held a stormy meeting before the vote was finally taken authorizing the statement. It had been necessary for me to go through previous hearings and to cite for the counsel a full list of situations in which witnesses had made statements. These citations involved both friendly and unfriendly witnesses. In the Hollywood hearings of 1947, a number of witnesses made initial statements, among them Sam Warner and Louis B. Mayer. Both Paul V. McNutt and Eric Johnston were permitted to read statements in that hearing at the beginning of their testimony. Albert Maltz, an unfriendly witness, was allowed to read such a statement. Whittaker Chambers almost immediately after taking the chair was given this opportunity. And Silvermaster too! Gerald L. K. Smith was permitted to read long sections from a statement, though not at the beginning. And yet a Bishop of a church who had requested a hearing for purposes of redress faced strenuous opposition when he insisted upon making a statement at the beginning of the session. Mr. Velde went out of his way to say, "It should be understood that this does not establish a precedent in the matter of written or oral statements and that the standard procedure of the Committee in this regard will be adhered to in all cases in the future." What did he mean by "standard procedure"? There are apparently no standards in the conduct of the business of this Committee, save only the caprice of its members.

One statement, however, of first importance was made by Mr. Velde. He said, "If the information contained in the Committee files is inaccurate or misleading, it should and will be corrected to reflect the truth or falsity of the data."

So far as I know, the files have not been corrected. Some members of the Committee have insisted that the record of the hearing is sufficient. It is not sufficient. If the files still contain falsehoods and if these files are to be released in the future, the facts that occasioned the hearing still remain. In a word, if a Congressional committee continues to broadcast material that defames, it becomes party to defamation of character. The counsel was particularly careful to point out that Mr. Parlin had received copies of the Rules of Procedure of the Committee, stating, "It is my understanding . . . that you fully understand the rules and the position of counsel in this Congressional hearing. Am I correct, sir?" Mr. Parlin replied, "I have received the rules, and I think I understand them." These rules had just been printed, and represent the first time that the Committee had printed anything in the way of rules—rules which, by the way, have subsequently been disregarded by the Committee itself.

After Mr. Velde's statement and my taking of the oath, Mr. Velde requested the members of the Committee not to interfere while I read the statement.

It was difficult to read under the circumstances of the hearing. A speaker is accustomed to looking an audience in the face, and seeks to appraise the impact of his statements upon the minds of the hearers. In this case, crowded in among journalists, somewhat blinded by television lights, aware of the counsel and his staff moving their papers about, eager to read in a calm and unhurried voice but under the pressure of a fifteen-minute time limit. I found myself under some little strain. The material was not new to the Committee, since their newly published rules required that statements be submitted twenty-four hours in advance. Nevertheless, I was naïve enough to hope that a calm statement might be meaningful. I got the impression, as I read, that some members of the Committee were listening with care.

◀ ‖ ▶

I protest against procedures that are in effect the rule of men and not the rule of law; procedures subject to the prejudices, passions and political ambitions of Committeemen; procedures designed less to elicit information than to entrap; procedures that cease to be investigation and become inquisition and intimidation.

IN WRITING the statement, I had tried to put the full purpose of my request into the first sentence: "Mr. Chairman and Members of the Committee, I have requested opportunity to appear voluntarily before this Committee, in public session, to secure redress for the damage done me by the release of information in the 'files' of this Committee." Mr. Parlin had suggested to me that I insert the next sentence, "I deeply appreciate the grant of this privilege." I agreed to that because it was a matter of courtesy, although I felt certain inhibitions in the matter of expressing appreciation to a group that had abused its privileges through the years and now required a citizen to come before the abusers in order to eliminate the abuse. I continued: "Such releases, made at various times for a period of nearly seven years, have contained material, much of which is irrelevant and immaterial, some of which is false and some of which is true, but all prepared in a way capable of creating the impression that I have been and am sympathetic to communism, and therefore subversive."

There is no question in my mind but that this material was deliberately slanted for no other purpose than to discredit. I am quite convinced that the techniques of Dr. J. B. Matthews, of Senator McCarthy, and men of this stripe, the techniques of Hitler or Goebbels, require a whipping boy. Who would have read the fantastic volume by Mrs. Elizabeth Dilling entitled *The Red Network* if it had not been an attack upon persons? Strangely enough, too many of us read such material with quickened heartbeat. This is a carry-over from savagery, and manifests itself in the hideous mob psychology of the lynching or in contemporary practices through which individuals are lynched by label. If the attack is to hold attention, it must be personalized. Therefore, individuals are singled out.

Why this Committee should have continued to release material which was demonstrably false, I do not know. I know that it did so; and now, in the reading of the statement, I hoped that before the day was over these matters could be cleared once and for all.

But I did not want to rest my case in simple refutation or in calling such men as Congressmen Velde and Jackson to account.

The issue to me was far deeper, and so with but fifteen minutes allotted, I turned to what I believed to be the fundamentals.

The room became silent. I said:

When I declare, "I believe in God, the Father Almighty," I affirm the theistic faith and strike at the fundamental fallacy of communism, which is atheism. I thereby reaffirm the basic conviction upon which this republic rests, namely, that all men are created by the Eternal and in His image, beings of infinite worth, members of one family, brothers. We are endowed by the Creator with certain inalienable rights. The State does not confer them; it merely confirms them. They belong to man because he is a son of God. When I say, "I believe in God," I am also saying that moral law is written into the nature of things. There are moral absolutes. Marxism, by definition, rules out moral absolutes. Because I believe the will of God is revealed in the Gospel of Christ, I hold that all historically conditioned political, economic, social, and ecclesiastical systems must be judged by the Gospel, not identified with it. This is to say I reject communism, first, because of its atheism.

There was a puzzled expression upon the faces of some Committeemen. I continued:

When I declare, "I believe in Jesus Christ, His only Son, our Lord," I am affirming faith in a spiritual view of life. By so doing, I repudiate the philosophy of materialism upon which communism is based, and thereby undermine it. I reject the theory of social development that assumes social institutions and even morality are determined by the prevailing mode of production. When I accept the law of love taught by Christ and revealed in His person, I must, of necessity, oppose to the death a theory that justifies dictatorship with its annihilation of freedom. I am not an economist, but have studied sufficiently to be convinced that there are basic fallacies in Marxian economics. Believing as I do that personality is a supreme good and that personality flowers in freedom, I stand for the free man in the free society, seeking the truth that frees. I hold that the free man must discover concrete measures through which the ideals of religion may be translated into the realities of world law and order, economic justice, and racial brotherhood.

As a result of long study and of prayer, I am by conviction pledged to the free way of life and opposed to all forms of totalitarianism, left or right, and to all tendencies toward such practices at home or abroad. Consequently, I have been actively opposed to communism all my life. I have never been a member of the Communist Party. My opposition to communism is a matter of public record in books, numerous articles, addresses, and sermons, and in resolutions I have drafted or sponsored in which powerful religious agencies have been put on record as opposed to communism. It is evidenced likewise in a life of service and the sponsorship of measures designed to make the free society impregnable to communist attack.

Loyalty to my family, my church, and my country are fundamental to me; and when any man or any Committee questions that loyalty, I doubt that I would be worthy of the name American if I took it lying down.

I then proceeded to certain considerations that I stated "I desire to lay before this Committee":

First, this Committee has followed a practice of releasing unverified and unevaluated material designated as "information" to citizens, organizations, and Members of Congress. It accepts no responsibility for the accuracy of the newspaper clippings recorded and so released; and insists that the material does not represent an opinion or a conclusion of the Committee. This material, officially released on official letterheads and signed by an official clerk, carried no disclaimer, in my case, and the recipient understandably assumed it did represent a conclusion. I am here formally to request that this "file" be cleaned up, that the Committee frankly admit its inaccuracies and misrepresentations, and that this matter be brought to a close.

It is alleged that the Committee has "files" on a million individuals, many of whom are among the most respected, patriotic, and devoted citizens of this nation. This is not the proper place to raise question as to the propriety of maintaining such vast "files" at public expense; but it is the proper place, in my case, to request that the practice of releasing unverified and unevaluated material, for which the Committee accepts no responsibility, cease. It can be shown that these reports are the result of inexcusable incompetence or of slanted selection, the result being the same in either case, namely, to question loyalty, to pillory or to intimidate the individual, to damage reputation, and to turn attention from the communist conspirator who pursues his nefarious work in the shadows, while a patriotic citizen is disgraced in public. The preparation and publication of these "files" puts into the hands of irresponsible individuals and agencies a wicked tool. It gives rise to a new and vicious expression of Ku-Kluxism, in which an innocent person may be beaten by unknown assailants who are cloaked in anonymity and at times immunity, whose whips are cleverly constructed lists of so-called subversive organizations and whose floggings appear all too often to be sadistic in spirit rather than patriotic in purpose.

I announced, "I had planned, at this point, to set forth specifications of what I believe is false," but the time allotted was insufficient for that purpose, and I therefore requested the Committee to question me upon certain issues.

It was apparent as the day progressed that the Committee had no intention of dealing with the files, as such. Again and again, I urged them to come to the specific questions that I had raised. New material had been dug up, probably in the hope that I might be made ridiculous in public and the Committee thereby exonerated.

The hearing had begun at two o'clock, but after midnight I was still asking the Committee to consider the items upon which I had requested them to question me.

I then took up one of the un-American practices of the Committee. In a debate with the Honorable Donald L. Jackson on the American Forum of the Air, Mr. Jackson had said, with reference to the files, "The Committee, in its work, accumulates all pertinent information relative to any given individual whose name is listed in the files. That is the only way by which one can determine the philosophical bent of any given individual." This was as false as the practice is vicious. Mr. Jackson knew perfectly well the Committee had done nothing of the kind. There is no attempt to get the philosophical bent of an individual. There is no attempt to accumulate all pertinent information. I asked, "Can the philosophy of an individual be determined by a scissors and paste process of cutting out clippings that damn? Why did the individual who clipped derogatory statements concerning me fail to clip such announcements as the following:

"My appointment by the Joint Chiefs of Staff to visit the Mediterranean Theater and the European Theater of Operations during the War; or my appointment by Secretary Forrestal as a member of the Secretary of the Navy's Civilian Advisory Committee; or the announcement that the Navy had awarded me the highly prized Certificate of Appreciation for services during the War; or that I had been invited to be the guest of Archbishop Damaskinos, then Regent of Greece, and that the King of Greece had awarded me the Order of the Phoenix; or that I had represented the American churches at the enthronement of the Archbishop of Canterbury; or that I had been appointed by the President as a member of the President's Commission on Higher Education; or that I was chairman of the Commission approved by the President to study postwar religious conditions in Germany? This might be called pertinent information. I have held the highest offices in the power of fellow-churchmen to confer upon me, such as the presidency of the Federal Council of the Churches of Christ in America. I am one of the Presidents of the World Council of Churches, perhaps the highest honor that can come to a clergyman. I hold positions of responsibility in the church I love and seek to serve, among them Secretary of the Council of Bishops."

It was embarrassing to recount all of this, but a Committee that would release a statement concerning me couched in the style of the "WANTED" announcements that appear in post offices, describing criminals who are at large, had to be answered in this fashion. One release of the Committee began, "G. Bromley Oxnam. This individual is a Methodist minister, and is sometimes referred to as a collectivist bishop."

I concluded that section with the statement:

We cannot beat down the Communist menace by bearing false witness against fellow Americans. The Communist wants a divided America, an America whose citizens are suspicious of each other, an America without trust, an America open to infiltration. I believe this Committee will wish to end a practice that plays into Communist hands.

The third section made a basic recommendation, namely, that "the so-called 'public files' be closed out." More recently, Committee members seeking to defend themselves for the inexcusable practice of releasing unverified and unevaluated material in the so-called public files had tried to point out that there is a distinction between "investigative files" and "public files." We were informed that the invesigative files are never released. Public files, we were told, contain only materials that are available to the public elsewhere. If that be so, why should public money be spent to assemble records upon a million individuals, if the former Chief Investigator Robert E. Stripling's proud boast represents the truth? I said:

It may at first seem drastic to propose that the so-called "public files" be closed out, but is there any need of any file other than the investigative files, as they have been recently described? Could not all the material that is of value in the public files be included in the investigative files? If, for purposes of education or exposure, the Committee decides that public statements must be made, is there any reason why a careful statement that will stand scrutiny cannot be made by studying the material in the investigative files? The Committee informs us that it does not vouch for the accuracy of the public files, that everything in those files is available to the public elsewhere. Why, then, should public money be spent in maintaining such public files? Would it not be well for the Committee to appoint a subcommittee to investigate its own files and those who compile them, and to secure answers to questions such as the following: How much duplication is there in the public and investigative files of this Committee and the files of the F.B.I.? Is the F.B.I. better equipped to get the facts on real subversives? Why was Appendix IX withdrawn from the public, and why is it under lock and key in the Library of Congress? Was it because of inexcusable inaccuracies and vicious slanting of material? How much of it is still the core of the public files? If there is real misunderstanding, would it not be well to ascertain who is misinforming whom and why?

It seemed to be necessary to call upon Mr. Jackson to apologize publicly for his unwarranted attack upon the House floor. This I did. I said:

I respectfully request Mr. Jackson to apologize on the floor of the House for his unprecedented and untrue statements made there concerning me. I will be the first to shake hands with him and to call the incident closed.

The statement concluded, as follows:

I believe the churches have done and are doing far more to destroy the Communist threat to faith and to freedom than all the investigating committees put together. I think the chairman of this Committee, after a friendly interview, concurred publicly in that statement when I made it in his presence. This Committee might well have the co-operation of millions of citizens who belong to the churches if it would cease practices that many of us believe to be un-American and would turn itself to the real task and the real threat. But those citizens will never co-operate in practices that jeopardize the rights of free men won after a thousand years' struggle for political and religious freedom. They will co-operate effectively with agencies everywhere that honestly seek to build the free society, where free men may worship God according to the dictates of conscience, and serve their fellow men in accordance with Christ's law of love.

I hardly concluded before Mr. Velde said, "I do regret that you did engage in personalities with a member of this Committee in violation of my instructions in my opening statement."

I replied that I had submitted my statement in advance, and that since Mr. Jackson was speaking upon the work of the Committee itself, I did not regard this as engaging in personalities, but in any case, if I had violated the rules, I said, "I hasten to apologize." Mr. Jackson stated that he took no personal exception.

It was quite apparent that Committee members had planned to introduce new material into the hearing. Mr. Velde said, "We do have some additional questions relative to some of the matters which are in your file and some of the matters which have been mentioned by you, and we, of course, as representatives of the American people, want to clear these up. I feel the only way for the Committee properly to understand the whole situation and for the record to be correct is to go into these matters throughly in this hearing today."

Mr. Kunzig then let the cat out of the bag by announcing that in the statement I had just read I had "made reference to a detailed reply" to the original report. I had made no such reference. He said, "I feel that in the interest of fairness and in the interest of creating a record which will present the full picture of all viewpoints concerning the matter being heard here today that we should incorporate into the record both the statement put out by the predecessors to this Committee and the answer which Bishop Oxnam has caused to be published." He therefore introduced into the record one of the releases of the Committee and the reply that I had made which had been published in the Washington *Post*. This was done quickly and quietly, and the large audience, as well as the great radio and television audience, heard none of my replies to the falsehoods that had been circulated by this Committee over a period of seven years.

Did this mean that the Committee accepted my answers? If so, why was I requestioned regarding some of the organizations I had not belonged to; did they hope by bringing in some alleged association to create the impression that I had falsified? We were there to examine the very files which by this artifice both the seen and unseen audience did not see. It was a stratagem at once crude and clever.

The counsel, knowing that I had belonged to the Massachusetts Council of American-Soviet Friendship and that I had sponsored the National Council of American-Soviet Friendship, Incorporated, began on what he thought to be firm ground. I had served as chairman of the Massachusetts Council.

Dates seemed to be meaningless to these individuals. For instance, men who are today calling for full co-operation with Western Germany which, under the circumstances, is probably a necessary if not a wise procedure, would find themselves in an embarrassing situation ten years from now if Germany, once again strong, should make war upon us. It would be possible to quote all of the statements urging friendship at a time utterly different. There is no willingness to understand the different time situations that we confront as the decades come and go. I tried to point this out:

Would you please note the dates. We were at war. Russia was one of our allies. I was approached in Boston, asked whether or not I would be interested in a small organization whose sole purpose would be to deepen friendship between the American and the Russian peoples. I stated I was interested in deepening such friendship. I was invited to address certain meetings. One was called the Salute to our Russian Ally. I think the date of that was November 8, 1942. I did address that meeting.

I then pointed out who were the sponsors of such a meeting, and referred only, because of the pressure of time, to Secretary and Mrs. Cordell Hull and to Lord and Lady Halifax. I mentioned that the other sponsors of that meeting were listed in the exhibit Mr. Kunzig introduced into the record: He said, "Yes, it is: I want to make it clear; it is in the record already."

Among the names I might have read were: The Honorable and Mrs. Joseph E. Davies, Secretary and Mrs. Jesse Jones, Administrator and Mrs. Paul V. McNutt, Assistant Secretary and Mrs. Breckinridge Long, Director and Mrs. E. R. Stettinius, Jr., Assistant Attorney General and Mrs. Thurman W. Arnold, Senator Arthur Capper, Senator Theodore F. Green, Senator Joseph F. Guffey, Senator Kenneth D. McKellar, Senator and Mrs. Claude D. Pepper, Van Wyck Brooks, Major George Fielding Eliot, Professor Albert Einstein, James W. Gerard, William Green, Sidney Hillman, Mr. and Mrs. Thomas W. Lamont, Thomas Mann, Fredric March, Robert A. Millikan, Philip Murray, Paul Robeson, Edward G. Robinson, Dorothy Thompson, William Allen White, Owen D. Young, Mayor and Mrs. Maurice J. Tobin, Governor and Mrs. Leverett Saltonstall, President and Mrs. K. T. Compton, Bishop Henry K. Sherrill, Professor and Mrs. Pitirim Sorokin. I stated, "I thought I was in excellent company. I thought I was doing a patriotic service. During the time that I served with that group, I believe no subversive act of any kind was committed by any individual related to it, and I believe no statement was made at any meeting that I know anything about that in any way would be questioned from the standpoint of patriotism."

I testified that my relation to this committee had really begun on April 6, 1943, and that I resigned as chairman of the Massachusetts group in August of 1943. I pointed out that in December of 1946 I noted that they were continuing my name as honorary chairman. I was then a resident of New York, having gone there in 1944. I wrote to the Massachusetts group, pointed out this fact, and requested that my name be discontinued.

At this point, Mr. Walter broke in, and asked, "Bishop, who asked you to join the Massachusetts organization?" I stated that Professor Dirk J. Struik had extended the invitation. Mr. Clardy, in rising inflection, spelled out the name ominously. The trap was set. The hunters awaited the unwary step. I said, "Yes, [Professor Struik] of the Massachusetts Institute of Technology, wrote suggesting that an organization be formed 'to promote Soviet-American friendship both during wartime and in the period of postwar reconstruction. A better mutual understanding of the two great peoples is not only necessary for victory, but is also a prerequisite for a lasting peace.' "

Mr. Walter pressed the matter, and asked, "Who is Professor Struik?"

I replied, "He was a professor in the Massachusetts Institute of Technology."

The record that follows indicates an attempt at the very beginning of the hearing to associate me with a person alleged to be a Soviet espionage agent. It is interesting to note that men trained in the law could state as Mr. Walter did state, "The fact of the matter is, this professor was a Russian spy, was he not?"

Mr. Kunzig wheeled up the "citation and identification" cannon which were to be fired all day. "They are the official identifications of Dirk J. Struik."

These men knew perfectly well that this man had not been tried; that he had never been found guilty. I have no brief for Professor Struik. I did what any reasonable man would do, namely, I inquired of the University and was informed that he was a distinguished professor of mathematics. He was a Dutchman. There was nothing in his conduct or conversation to indicate that he was a Communist. Naturally, there would not be, if he were an espionage agent. These committeemen had made up their minds before the accused had been tried. It is one of the attitudes prevalent in the conduct of these hearings. Because somebody once a Communist has identified a man as a member of the Party, he by that accusation or identification is thereby proved guilty. He is put in the place of having to prove that he is not something that someone else alleges he is. It is the direct reversal of the American approach.

It was clear what was going on. The Committee was trying to undermine me at the very beginning of the hearing. I therefore said, "I realize the impression that is being created here, Mr. Chairman, by this kind of procedure. I could read at this moment into the record, if you will allow me, a statement by General Dwight D. Eisenhower to the National Council of this organization, dated November, 1945, which reads: 'American-Soviet friendship is one of the cornerstones—' " Mr. Velde broke in, and stated, "Just a minute, Bishop, I think we have been overly fair in granting you the privilege of making a statement."

I was not making a statement. I was trying to indicate the kind of organization with which I had co-operated. It was apparent that Mr. Velde was perfectly willing to allow the introduction of derogatory material, but the moment I sought to present additional pertinent data he spoke of granting me a "privilege." An investigating committee ought to be interested in facts.

Fortunately, Mr. Doyle broke in, and said, "Mr. Chairman, I object to that ruling by the Chairman. I think this witness ought to be privileged to read that statement by the President of the United States." Mr. Velde gave in, and said, "All right." I then said, "This was a message to the National Council, dated November, 1945, from the then General Dwight D. Eisenhower." I read the message:

American-Soviet friendship is one of the cornerstones on which the edifice of peace should be built. To achieve this friendship, nothing is more important than mutual understanding on the part of each of the institutions, traditions, and customs of the other. As an American soldier and lover of peace, I wish your Council the utmost success in the worthy work it has undertaken.

When I had finished reading this, I said, "Mr. Chairman, my relationship, I trust, was of similar nature and similar spirit."

Mr. Velde said somewhat grudgingly, "Certainly you should introduce anything that you want to, but my request was that you answer the questions that were put to you by counsel as closely to the subject matter as possible." I wondered what Mr. Velde meant. Was I to walk into the trap set up by this Committee? Or was I to present the facts that would make the situation understandable?

Mr. Clardy was unwilling to let the matter rest at that. It was clear that the reading of the letter from the President had had profound effect upon those present in the hearing room and no doubt upon the radio audience. So Mr. Clardy said, "Bishop, as I understand it, you were asked into the organization by Professor Struik without knowing anything about his background or his Communist connection, as I get it?"

I replied, "Mr. Clardy, when he came to see me or wrote this letter, I had never heard of him. I did the only thing, I think, that a person would normally do. I did have my secretary phone the university to find out who he was. The answer was the answer I reported a few moments ago. . . . I suppose we met a few times. I do not know the man, and if it be he is involved, as has been suggested here, I regret the association far more than I can express."

Mr. Clardy then went on to show that the Committee had discovered that Professor Struik was a Communist. He said, "I am sorry we did not discover it before you had that association because I am sure you would not have associated with it, had you known it."

The waste of public money in procedures such as this is clearly seen as the hearing develops. It would have been a simple matter for this Committee to have sent one of its representatives to see me back in 1946 or at any time over a period of seven years. This was never done. All of this material could have been examined and a correct record made. No one came. Had the F.B.I. been conducting an investigation, an agent would have called; the facts would have been made available; and the record made perfectly clear.

After beginning with the attempt to associate me with an espionage agent, the Committee then took its next step. It was apparent they had failed, because of the quotation from President Eisenhower. There was no recognition of the fact that I had resigned from this organization, in which, so far as I knew, no subversive act of any kind had occurred. We had rendered, I think, valuable service at a time when friendship between the American and the Russian peoples was necessary. I had offered a prayer at a great meeting at Madison Square Garden in New York, which was subsequently read by Jane Cowl on her radio program.

When a committee circulates statements to the effect that a citizen is a member of an organization, refrains from indicating that he resigned and when he resigned, and does so with no reference to the situation the member confronted at the time of membership, what is its purpose?

The following quotations from messages written to or delivered by individuals who participated in rallies under the auspices of the

National Council of American-Soviet Friendship in 1944 and 1945 are significant. For instance:

I am grateful to you and all those who are celebrating American-Soviet Friendship Day for the words of support and confidence I have received. There is no better tribute we can hold out to our allies than to continue working in ever-growing accord to establish a peace that will endure. The Dumbarton Oaks Conference was a step in this direction. Other steps will be taken. In line with this objective, such meetings as you are holding in Madison Square Garden and in other great centers throughout the United States are of tremendous assistance and value.

This was signed by Franklin Delano Roosevelt.

It was at this meeting that I offered prayer. It is stated that twenty thousand people were present in Madison Square Garden. Among those present and speaking were Acting Secretary of State Edward R. Stettinius, Jr., and the British Ambassador, the Earl of Halifax. American industry was represented by Henry J. Kaiser, American labor by Philip Murray, president of the Congress of Industrial Organizations, William Green, president of the American Federation of Labor, and A. F. Whitney, president of the Brotherhood of Railway Trainmen. Dr. Serge Koussevitzky, chairman of the Music Committee of the National Council of American-Soviet Friendship, brought a message. Messages were received from General Dwight D. Eisenhower, Lt. Gen. Jacob L. Devers, and Lt. Gen. A. M. Patch. The Secretary of the Interior Harold L. Ickes addressed the Madison Square Garden meeting of 1943.

The Earl of Halifax, British Ambassador to the United States, said:

I am very glad to be here tonight . . . to pay my tribute of respect and admiration to a great fighting ally. . . . I am the more happy to do this on the day when you celebrate the eleventh anniversary of the establishment of relations between the United States and the Soviet Union. That was an event of the first importance. For the good relations of 300 million people, who have so much to gain and nothing to lose from their friendship, means a lot to the world.

Speaking of Germany, he said:

She will do all she can to foster misunderstandings, to induce us to question one another's motives, to suspect one another's purposes, to suggest that in some way each one of us is out to get the better of the other. That is an old Nazi habit. . . . That, I believe, is where the work of such a Council as this is so valuable. This society for the promotion of American-Soviet Friendship speaks for two sides of the triangle. The third side is the British Commonwealth; and it is symbolic of this three-fold association that the United States, Soviet Russia, and the British Commonwealth are represented here tonight. . . . We have run a long way together, and what we have so far been able to do is of good augury for the future. By still standing side by side, as we have stood in the dark days of the war, we shall not only win the object for which we now fight, we shall be doing what lies within human power to insure that the sacrifices and sufferings of this present time shall not have been in vain.

Why does the Committee on Un-American Activities fail to tell the American people what the spirit and the intent of such meetings really were? Why does it suggest conspiracy and co-operation with conspirators? Were the President of the United States and the British Ambassador conspirators?

Mrs. Winston Churchill sent a greeting to that meeting. She said:

It gives me great pleasure to send greetings to all those assembled tonight in Madison Square Garden to do honor to American-Soviet Friendship. On the friendship and mutual understanding between the United Nations rest the hopes of men for a peaceful and prosperous world. Let the peoples of the U.S.A., the U.S.S.R., and the British Commonwealth unite their efforts to that end, in peace and in war.

From Field Marshal Jan Christian Smuts, Prime Minister of the Union of South Africa, came word:

My warm good wishes for a most successful meeting. . . . Let this greatest of world wars be also the last.

Acting Secretary of State Edward R. Stettinius, Jr., said:

It is an honor for me to have this opportunity afforded by the Council of American-Soviet Friendship, to speak this evening on the close relationship existing between the United States and the Union of Soviet Socialist Republics. The friendship between our two countries is a cherished heritage of our peoples.

He concluded by saying:

My friend, Ambassador Gromyko, allow me, on behalf of the President and the Secretary of State, to convey to you, and through you to the government and the people of the Soviet Union, the cordial and warm regard of the American people and its government; our appreciation of the friendship which exists between us; and our confidence that there is in store for our nations, and for all the United Nations, a future of settled peace and of precious opportunity—such as the world has never known before—to advance the freedom and the well-being of all mankind.

The fact that these hopes were dashed to pieces upon the rocks of Communist duplicity should no more be held against those who sought co-operation at that time than the betrayal in Berlin that necessitated the air lift should be held against the American forces who had fought as allies of the Russian forces when we sought to destroy the Hitler threat to freedom.

Secretary of War Henry L. Stimson said:

Throughout the war, the heroic struggle of the Russian people against the Nazi aggressor has won the admiration of every freedom-loving nation. This mass meeting, called to celebrate the founding of the Soviet state as well as the opening of relations between our two governments, coincides with a great military triumph: the final liberation of all Russian soil from the invader. This happy result has been accomplished not only by the skill and fortitude of the red army but by the devotion of the entire Soviet people, civilian as well as military, to one single purpose.

Are we to witness the serving of subpoenas upon all those who joined in these sincere, honest attempts to deepen friendship between the two peoples? Roosevelt, Smuts, Stettinius, Stimson and Ickes are dead. Are their names to be dishonored as were the names of distinguished religious leaders by unverified testimony taken in executive session and released by this Committee without any regard for the reputations of the deceased or their families?

Is the Committee ready to take on Field Marshal Sir Bernard L. Montgomery? He also sent a greeting. Said he:

I send to the National Council of American-Soviet Friendship my greetings on the occasion of your meeting which the British Ambassador will address. At the present time, when the end of the war is in sight, it is more important than ever that the three great nations who have been responsible for the defeat of Germany should continue in close co-operation to design the post-war world.

Is Henry J. Kaiser to be pilloried today because at that time he said:

In spite of misunderstanding and perplexity, the United States of America and the Union of Soviet Socialist Republics have come to believe in each other through working together. Such faith is the cornerstone of the new world.

Are we to condemn the late Philip Murray, patriot and Roman Catholic, who did so much to drive communism from the ranks of labor in the United States, because he, too, said:

The C.I.O. therefore heartily welcomes your constructive efforts for closer Soviet-American friendship, and I hope your meeting will be successful in promoting this splendid purpose.

And is the late William Green, Baptist, president of the American Federation of Labor, whose staunch Americanism is known by all, to be castigated because he said:

In order to achieve our common objective, we must all serve in a determined way to maintain freedom, unity, good will, and understanding between the United States and Soviet Russia.

Are we to list the late Frank Murphy, Associate Justice of the

Supreme Court, among the subversives because on that occasion he wrote:

On this anniversary occasion, along with other Americans, I express gratitude to the soldiers of the Soviet Armies for the sacrifices they have made on the field of battle, sacrifices which have meant the saving of lives of American soldiers. It is my hope that the peoples of America and of the Union of Soviet Socialist Republics may always be actuated by impulses of friendship and kindness in their relationship with each other.

Must Field Marshal Sir Henry Maitland Wilson, Chief, the British Joint Staff Mission, come with his Field Marshal's baton in hand, bowing before this Committee in order to have his record cleared? He said:

When I first received your kind invitation to be your guest tonight and to say a few words, I asked a British colleague what I ought to say to an American audience. He replied: You must make some understatements. Americans always expect that of Englishmen. Well, I will not disappoint you. I will start by telling you that I regard it as a great privilege to be here. . . . In saluting the Red Army and its brilliant leader, Marshal Stalin, at the moment when it is approaching its greatest triumph, it is perhaps appropriate to remind ourselves that the triumph will have been hardly won and most richly deserved.

The utter absurdity of the continuing release of a statement that an individual was a sponsor of the National Council of American-Soviet Friendship for purposes of questioning his patriotism must be clear. Why does this Committee do this? Is it because it cannot ferret out the real Communist menace? Does it have to drum up support for the passing of appropriation bills so that it can continue its staff in office? Has the Committee ever checked upon its so-called researchists to ascertain who is misinforming whom? Has it ever thought of employing competent researchists, thoroughly familiar with the Communist movement, untainted by membership in the Communist Party?

◀ III ▶

I protest against the inexcusable incompetency that has characterized too many members of the research staff of the House Committee on Un-American Activities, an incompetency that has both duped and embarrassed members of the Committee.

NOW came the second attempt to discredit. The purpose, of course, was to make it appear that I had falsified. Mr. Kunzig, putting on an act, said, "Sir, I am puzzled here in one respect. You stated that you were active in this group, in the National Council and in the Massachusetts Council, and you stated that in your reply published in a daily newspaper here in Washington, and yet in 1946, in the Knoxville *Journal*, is published a letter you wrote to a Reverend Cooper in which you had been accused of being a member of these various organizations, among which was the one we are now discussing, and your answer at that time was, 'As a matter of fact, I never belonged to the organizations mentioned, except the American Civil Liberties Union, and know nothing about most of them.' I just do not understand how you could say that you never belonged when you were talking in 1946 and in 1953 you say that you did."

A franked envelope would have carried this inquiry to my office and would have elicited the reply that I then gave. Mr. Kunzig need not have been puzzled so long.

I stated, "I can explain it very easily, Mr. Kunzig. . . . I receive from fifty to one hundred letters every day. It is something of a

chore to answer them every morning. I have been plagued through
the years by these lists that have come in from Mrs. Elizabeth Dilling,
the American Council of Christian Laymen, and the like, asking, 'Do
you or do you not belong to this or the other?' This minister of the
Methodist Church wrote me a letter because I was announced to
speak at the Tennessee State Teachers Association at Knoxville. . . .
I was going there to see my friend, Mr. David E. Lilienthal, and this
letter came with a list of them. I dictated an answer, and I am very
sorry; I made a mistake in that. I said . . . 'as a matter of fact I have
never belonged.' Is that not what the statement is? I said, 'I have
never belonged to any of these organizations except the American
Civil Liberties Union.' "

Mr. Kunzig replied, "Yes."

I then said, "Now, as a matter of fact, there were two or three
organizations there to which I had belonged. I noted that within a
few days, and I wrote that minister and made a correction to read,
'I do not belong to any of these organizations except the American
Civil Liberties Union.' " And that was the way the matter rested.

Mr. Jackson was unwilling to let the matter rest. He said, "Bishop,
I realize a considerable period of time has elapsed since your communication with the gentleman in Knoxville. Do your files contain
those letters, which might be incorporated?"

I replied, "I wish they did, Mr. Jackson. I have moved, and when
a Bishop moves he usually has a very large file to deal with. If you
receive fifty to one hundred letters a day, you are dealing with 25,000
letters a year, perhaps, and in five years it is an immense file. When
I left Boston, I cleared those files, keeping the matters that had to
do with character problems, property, and the like. Similarly, when
I left New York. I hoped I had this file. I found that I did not. I
telephoned this minister, and I asked him—or rather, I had my
secretary telephone him and ask him if he had these letters. He said
he did have the letters and would send them to me. He sent one of

them. I phoned him again, and asked for the other. He tells me he will try to find the other, and I hope to be able to make it a matter of record."

Mr. Jackson then said, "If you do receive them, would you be kind enough to let the Committee have them?"

On August 22, 1953, the Reverend D. B. Cooper addressed a letter to the Reverend T. Otto Nall, editor of *The Christian Advocate*, the official paper of the Methodist Church, in response to an inquiry that Dr. Nall had made concerning this matter. Mr. Cooper said:

Dear Brother Nall:

In reference to your inquiry of the two letters Bishop Oxnam wrote me in 1946, I do not have them.

The first letter I found and returned to Bishop Oxnam, but the second letter was evidently lost, as I cannot find it in my files.

"Why did Bishop Oxnam write me then?" The Knoxville *Journal* was attacking him frequently in 1946. Copies of these letters I, of my own accord, sent Bishop Oxnam, that he might know about it. He, of course, naturally wrote to thank me, and in the first letter he made a statement which I read to the Knoxville District Ministers' Meeting. The Knoxville *Journal*, a few hours later, phoned me, requesting this letter for publicity. I refused to let them have it, but allowed them to quote me as to the content of letter. That they published the following Sunday, perhaps in October, 1946.

Bishop Oxnam wrote me a second letter immediately, on seeing quotation in Knoxville *Journal* from his first letter, correcting his first letter. I read this to the same Knoxville District Ministers' Meeting (Methodist). I do not know whether it was published in either Knoxville *Journal* or Knoxville *Sentinel*. If they asked me for it, I would have given them the information, but I was not seeking publicity nor appointed by Bishop Oxnam to speak for him. All Journals referring to Bishop Oxnam were sent him by me for his information.

Bishop Oxnam's second letter of correction said in effect: "I do not belong to any of these organizations except the American Civil Liberties Union."

Any additional statement should come from Bishop Oxnam. We appreciate your defense of him, whom we regard as the greatest leader in Methodism and Protestantism today.

Very sincerely yours,

(Signed) D. B. Cooper.

Fries, Virginia
August 22, 1953.

Is it necessary for an investigating committee with a paid research staff to be so ill-informed? When a committeeman asks such a question through counsel, as was done that day, was there any other purpose than to question my veracity? The important point here is this: How many Americans are being maligned by this process? How many Americans possess such standing among their friends that such an attack fails to ostracize them? Some members of this Committee have deliberately sought by such exposure to impoverish the accused and to ostracize him. He is impoverished because the exposure results in the loss of his job. He is ostracized because too many have believed too much unfounded rumor publicized at public expense by a few.

Thus far in the hearing, two attempts had been made to discredit me: one, the attempt to make it appear that association with the Council for American-Soviet Friendship was subversive. Honesty would have called for a statement of the service of that organization and of the outstanding Americans who had co-operated with it; but the Committee was content to suggest association with an alleged espionage agent. The other was an attempt to prove that my word could not be relied upon. Both of these attempts, I think, blew up in their faces.

◀ IV ▶

I protest against the release of unverified and unevaluated material from the so-called files of this Committee on official letterhead and signed by an official clerk, a practice particularly reprehensible since the Committee refuses to vouch for the accuracy of the material and insists it does not represent an opinion or a conclusion of the Committee. The alleged inclusion of a disclaimer, disavowing responsibility or accuracy, is no justification for the release of falsehood because to release it is in effect to validate it.

THEN, without a moment's warning, Mr. Kunzig said, "You undoubtedly know that the National Council of American-Soviet Friendship grew out of Friends of the Soviet Union, another cited organization by the Attorney General of the United States of America, and that came originally from Friends of Soviet Russia, another one of these organizations. Do you recall whether, as is stated in the Los Angeles *Times*—I am going back now to Thursday morning, April 26, 1923—do you recall whether you spoke—"

The audience roared in derision. Here was a man going back thirty years and asking me if I recalled whether I spoke at a certain meeting.

As a matter of fact, the record lacks clarity here, because Mr. Kunzig's first question dealt with April 26, 1923; but when the laughter of the audience had subsided and Mr. Velde, incensed, had restored order, Mr. Kunzig, instead of dealing with that date, jumped to August 30, 1922. I thought he was still referring to 1923 and to

a reproduction of a dodger that had appeared in the Los Angeles
Times. I exhibited a bound volume containing a record of my activities in 1923, and stated, "I never authorized my name for that meeting. I did not appear at that meeting. I therefore did not speak at that
meeting." I made reference to a letter of protest that I had addressed
to the Los Angeles *Times*, and said, "If you wish me to take the time,
I will find the letter and read it."

Mr. Velde requested that I insert this in the record rather than take
time to read it.

Mr. Kunzig seemed to be confused. There was some question as to
date. He said August 30, 1922. I asked him whether it was 1922 or
1923, and he then said 1923.

I pointed out that this material had never been released from the
files in any release that I had seen. Mr. Doyle broke in, "May I ask,
as a member of the Committee, is this incident something about which
there has been no release and about which the Bishop has had no
previous information from the Committee, or is it something about
which he has had previous information from the Committee? I would
like to know that myself."

Mr. Kunzig's answer was evasive. As a matter of fact, this material
had never been released.

Mr. Jackson, in his suave fashion, interjected, "I am confident that
the Bishop has no objection to answering any question to any material that may be related to the subject matter today. That is the only
way that this matter is going to be resolved. If information which
was not contained in the public files is information which might in
the future sometime cause embarrassment, I think that we are in
agreement, or at least I assume that we should be, on getting it
straightened out at this time. Whether or not it was contained in the
original report or not . . ."

I interrupted, and asked, "Do you wish me to answer that, Mr.
Chairman."

Mr. Velde said, "May I ask you, are you willing to answer questions regarding any of these organizations that you belonged to in the past?"

I replied, "Mr. Chairman, I came to get the files, as released, corrected, but I am very eager to have anything that anybody can bring up at any time during my life that anybody thinks is necessary to be brought out so that this matter can be cleared up once and for all. It is extremely embarrassing, sir, to have these matters released and then reprinted by private agencies to the damage of one's reputation. Therefore, my answer to you, sir, is, 'Of course.' "

Mr. Velde then thanked me for my co-operation.

The introduction of this material from thirty years ago caused Mr. Walter to ask, "What possible bearing can certain of these matters have on what we are doing here today?"

Mr. Velde said, "I think we can answer that question. We are attempting to straighten out the record for the Bishop, at his request, and anything that is favorable or unfavorable or that reflects what we are doing at the present time in the operation and the organization of Congress, and certainly it should be in the record."

Mr. Moulder then said, "I reserve the right to object to this."

Instead of clearing up the whole California situation, Mr. Kunzig then turned back to the present. It was in the evening that he was to raise a question again going back some thirty years. He referred to what he called a "document" which "refers to a mass meeting in which it lists two speakers, back in the early 1920's in Los Angeles, Harriet Dunlop Prenter, a well-known Communist, and yourself, Rev. G. Bromley Oxnam. Did you make a speech with this well-known Communist, or perhaps it lies beyond your recollection?"

I replied, "No, sir, it does not lie beyond my recollection." I asked him to pardon me for a moment. I wanted to get the material at hand. I said, "You see, Mr. Chairman, this is what I am getting at. This material of over thirty years ago has been used again and again and again, and here it is in 1953 coming back. Fortunately, this is something upon which I can deal. There is a dodger which should have been shown, which alleges that I was to speak at a certain place. No doubt the counsel has this. Fortunately,—" Mr. Kunzig broke in, "There it is, sir." I said, "Well, there it is. I have the same one." I then quoted from a letter dated April 29, 1921. It was a letter I had addressed to Bishop Adna Wright Leonard who had made inquiry concerning the dodger under discussion. In the letter to Bishop Leonard, I quoted in full a letter addressed to Mr. Louis Allen, 2117 Adair Street, Los Angeles, dated April 11, 1921. It was he who had extended an invitation to me to address that meeting.

Dear Sir:

In view of the fact that I distinctly told you I would not speak at the general amnesty meeting if it were in any way associated with the IWW, or if the name "class-war prisoners" was used, I find it will be impossible for me to speak for you.

I have just seen the dodgers you sent out, in which the object of the meeting is distinctly stated as calling for the freedom of class-war prisoners.

My position was clearly enough stated to you—namely, that I did not favor the freeing of any man who broke the law. I am in favor of freeing conscientious objectors, who committed no crime other than refusing to take arms contrary to their convictions. I think you are making a bad mistake in putting both groups in the same class.

Thank you for the books you sent me. I shall read all of them. Will you kindly send me a bill?

Very truly yours,
(Signed) G. Bromley Oxnam.

After reading the letter, I looked directly at Mr. Velde and said, "Now, sir, it's just my good fortune that I happen to have that letter. If you asked me without this, I would have to say I don't recall. That's the embarrassing place in which an individual is put in these matters. I was not at that meeting—I answer your counsel—and I was not at it for the reason I have never co-operated with people who talk in terms of class-war prisoners. A man who conscientiously believes that he can't bear arms—I've disagreed with him; I've never held the pacifist view, but I respect him if he's honest, and my Government does; and that meeting was pointed out to me as a meeting for the release of conscientious objectors. When I found it wasn't, I wrote the letter to which I have just referred.

"And that is my answer, sir, to that matter."

Mr. Velde replied, "The Committee appreciates you are able to explain that incident in that manner."

I wondered.

How many people are able to produce a letter thirty years old relative to such a matter? The intent of the counsel's question was to suggest that I had associated with subversives thirty years ago. It should be noted that Mrs. Prenter is referred to as "a well-known Communist." There is no proof introduced that she was a Communist, but the counsel not only described her as "a well-known Communist" but in the question he put to me, he said, "Did you make a speech with this well-known Communist?"

In recounting the story in proper sequence, I must point out that Mr. Kunzig would jump from 1953 back to 1923 and back again. To elicit the facts, it would appear reasonable to complete one period at one time. What purpose did such thirty-year jumps serve?

Reference was made to a circular announcing a meeting that I was alleged to have addressed in Los Angeles. Their "staff" had let them down again.

Mr. Kunzig said, "Here is one, sir, involving the IWW, which was a cited Communist group. It lists 'Protest mass meeting against the Criminal Syndicalism Act at Symphony Hall, 232 South Hill Street, February the 11th,' in that period of time, in 1923. It lists Rev. G. B. Oxnam, speaking together with members of the IWW. Did you speak at that group and did you work with the IWW?"

The counsel for the Committee appeared to have little knowledge of the difference between syndicalism and communism. I said, "I'll be happy to answer that, sir. I did not speak at that meeting. I never worked with the IWW."

I continued, "I have been a university professor, and have lectured in the field of the comparative study of the labor movements of the world. The IWW, which is really a part of the Syndicalist movement, has advocated, for instance, as one of its weapons, the use of sabotage. Sabotage for them was striking when they were on the job. I don't know whether the chairman wishes me to go into this. It would take a considerable period of time. I'll simply say I never had anything to do with the IWW. This incident, however, raises a very important question, Mr. Chairman. . . . I would very much like to answer this, because I don't want any doubt left in this record concerning the matter. I can answer it briefly, I think, and would like to read from the record, too. I think perhaps—"

Mr. Velde said, "The chair would appreciate it if you would."

My public opposition to syndicalism and to the IWW was well known in Los Angeles.

I said, because I had publicly condemned the IWW philosophy and method, a Mrs. Kate Crane Gartz, a wealthy woman of left-wing persuasion, wrote me a letter criticizing me for my public condemnation of the IWW. In a letter to Mrs. Gartz, dated June 5, 1923, I wrote:

"Now, as to the IWW, you suggest I be specific. Neither space nor time permits. A brief word, though: I have carefully read most of the literature of this movement prior to the war. You cannot deny that literature did teach the use of force as a legitimate method to attain the new industrial day. You cannot deny that official publications did advocate the use of sabotage, nor can you deny that such methods were used. . . . I, therefore, have been and am opposed to its philosophy and tactics. . . .

"Now, I know that since the war and the coming of the Criminal Syndicalist Act there has not been an official advocacy of force. In fact, I have been informed again and again the IWW repudiates force. Perhaps I am unjust, but I have felt this repudiation was rather a matter of expediency than conviction since the other method was justified but a short time since.

"I do not want to do any group an injustice, but so far I have not been able to change my mind on this matter. My mind is not closed, but so far the data available have not changed it."

I lifted my eyes and said, "I think Mr. Chairman, reading from the record at that time, in response to a person who criticized me for criticizing the IWW, that I have made it abundantly clear what my view was then and is now. The whole idea of sabotage is funda- mentally—"

Before I could finish, Mr. Walter broke in, and said, "At that time you were all of twenty-one years of age?"

The purpose of the question was pitifully obvious. I thought it implied that I was misinforming the Committee and had actually written that material later. Since Mr. Walter's arithmetic was faulty, I thought it easier to point that out than to reply to his insinuation, so I said, "No; I was more than that, sir—1923 plus nine would make me thirty-two, I think."

Mr. Clardy interrupted, and asked, "Don't you think the procedure we are following in exploring these things so you may clear the record is the best service we can perform for you?"

I replied, "Mr. Clardy, I appreciate that question and the spirit that lies back of it. Frankly, I think the best service that could be rendered to me as an individual, and to all the citizens of the United States, would be to see that these files are evaluated and verified before they are released to anybody."

MR. CLARDY: "Well, may I interrupt you? I am not talking about the general thing, I am talking about your own file that has been laid out to the public. Now, there are some things—and you made state- ments that you knew everything that was in the files. You really didn't, as you have already demonstrated here, and we are bringing those things in, too. So, my question is: Don't you think that the best course that we could follow in your self-interest would be to do exactly what we have been doing? If you tell me otherwise, I might be inclined to go along and suggest that we just desist."

BISHOP OXNAM: "Well, Mr. Clardy, if I express my opinion frankly—when a citizen finds files are released that he believes misrepresent him, it would seem to me, instead of going through all this, which has taken a day of the Committee—"

MR. CLARDY: "But you asked for it."

BISHOP OXNAM: "I did, but you are asking me what would be ideal—that it would be much better to allow an individual to come over here, or somebody to come over, to see the man and to check the files before they are released. Now, you say, sir, I referred to items that you never heard of."

MR. CLARDY: "Yes."

BISHOP OXNAM: "I have before me the file that was released by Mr. John S. Wood, the chairman of this Committee—not only to me, but to others—and from that file I listed the items, and if, sir, we could have begun—and it is presumptuous for me to suggest it as a Committee procedure, and I am not doing that; I am answering your question—if I could have had opportunity to have stated to the Committee what I believe to be incorrect in the files that I know have been released, we could have cleared that, I think, quickly. Then if the Committee wanted to subject me to questions concerning all of these questions, of course, I must stand that because I have requested the privilege of coming, and you have full right to know concerning everything else. That, it seems to me, would have been a little easier; but what you are driving at, sir, I agree and I appreciate."

MR. CLARDY: "Thank you."

One never knew which side of the fence Mr. Walter was coming down on. He was unpredictable. He said, "Don't you think we ought to treat this so-called raw information just as does the Department of Justice treat the same kind of information? It is information that ought not to be released."

I replied, "Yes, sir; I agree with you thoroughly; and it is because

I think in my case and in others that this kind of information has been released that I am petitioning the Committee to clear my own file and that of others—involving the National Council of the Churches of Christ, for instance. It has surprised me to find that this Committee would release a file headed, 'The National Council of the Churches of Christ in America,' but it has."

MR. WALTER: "That is the kind of information that is for the benefit of the members of the Committee solely, to evaluate as we see fit."

BISHOP OXNAM: "Yes, sir: I think you're exactly right."

MR. WALTER: "—without reaching any conclusion at all with respect to it. It has always seemed to me that we ought to evaluate it in our own concept and use it in connection with our own reports, but not as it relates to individuals."

BISHOP OXNAM: "I would not be here, sir, if that had been the practice of the Committee, and I appreciate what you say, and agree with it."

MR. WALTER: "Well, nobody agrees with me, ever."

BISHOP OXNAM: "Well, I am agreeing with you, sir."

At one point, controversy developed in the Committee itself. Mr. Jackson admitted that some of the material introduced that day had been "developed" by himself, and said, "The time element involved was such that it was not possible to get photostats made for each member of the Committee."

This is a clear admission of the introduction of new material into the record. I had asked for the revision of the record as it was at the time I demanded a hearing. Mr. Jackson, I suppose, had "developed" the material which was introduced, I take it, for the purpose of discrediting. Mr. Clardy stated at this point, "You have listed some items in your opening statement that, as a member of the Committee, I have never heard of in all the time I have been on the Committee, and I have interrogated all the rest of the members and they never

heard of them either." It is a strange fact that a statement I had read
at the beginning of the hearing and which had not been available
more than twenty-four hours to anyone had been so studied by Mr.
Clardy that he had interrogated all the members of the Committee
and they stated they had never heard of the items.

Mr. Kunzig, having begun with references to the American-Soviet
Friendship and then having questioned my veracity by quoting from
a newspaper back in 1946, hopped from one decade to another, and
suddenly dropped upon a meeting of the Arts, Sciences, and Progressive Citizens of America.

I interrupted, and said, "I had hoped you were going to deal with
the items to which I referred."

Mr. Kunzig brushed this off, and referred to a clipping from
The Daily Worker, entitled, "Leaders in Arts and Sciences Hit Pix
Purge." He proceeded to indicate that this organization had been
cited by the California Committee on Un-American Activities. In
other words, he was trying to make the picture as black as possible
by what was direct discourse.

I interrupted, saying, "I have not heard a question. Excuse me."

"The question," he replied, "The question is, were you associated
with these groups in any way, would you explain it so our records
would be clear?"

I replied that I had no recollection of any association with that
group whatsoever. His questions had been so confused that I had to
say, "It isn't quite clear in my mind what he is talking about."

Congressman Frazier broke in, "We are unable to determine from
counsel's question as to what organization the Bishop is being charged
with being a member of."

Mr. Jackson said, "As I understand, Bishop, you have no recollection of that."

I replied, "I have no recollection at all, and if the chair will not
think me violating the rules, it is precisely this which troubles me.

This kind of thing gets into these files, and without having been verified or checked, it goes out. I have no recollection of any association with that whatsoever."

It was at this point that Mr. Velde made a statement that is of fundamental importance. He said, "In the files that we have are reports which are already public information. *Any citizen can file them.*" Later, some members were to deny that this was true, but here is the chairman himself at an official hearing stating that any citizen can file the reports. This means that citizens with ulterior ends or organizations seeking to destroy can send information into the House Committee on Un-American Activities. They can then report that this material is in the files. Mr. Velde himself acknowledges that "any citizen can file them."

Some months before I did an interesting television show for the Columbia Broadcasting Company. One of the writers who does a thrilling detective story for Columbia was assigned the task of doing the script for the Sunday afternoon in which I was to participate. I told him about this procedure of the Committee. He, with a mind accustomed to dealing with detective stories, laughed and said, "That's an idea. I may use it some day."

This means, said the script writer, that a man who wanted to blackmail could send material to the House Committee on Un-American Activities. He could make it as black as he wanted to. He could then go to the person involved and state, "I know that the following information concerning you is in the files of the House Committee on Un-American Activities. Pay up, or I shall inform your employer." This is the basis of the blackmail. Thus a blackmailer who had sent in blackmail information blackmails an individual who has no knowledge that the falsehoods are even in the files, but, as Mr. Velde says, "Any citizen can file them."

It is a strange fact that a quotation from *The Daily Worker* alleging that an individual appeared at a certain place is taken at face value, but an allegation in *The Daily Worker* concerning members of the Committee is immediately discounted as "communist line." Several times during the hearing, quotations from *The Daily Worker* were introduced as though such information had come from Olympus or Sinai.

Mr. Kunzig then took up the American League Against War and Fascism. The Committee had repeatedly released an allegation of considerable linage to the effect that I had sponsored a meeting, which according to a statement in *The Daily Worker* had been held at Madison Square Garden, under the auspices of the League Against War and Fascism and the American Friends of the Chinese People. It was a meeting to be addressed by Ambassador William E. Dodd of Germany. Once again, how much more American it would have been for this Committee to have called and to have ascertained facts instead of releasing a lie for years and later of taking the time of the whole Committee and its staff at heavy public expense to ascertain facts easily available to anybody who really wanted them.

My reply in this connection follows:

I had no association with the American League Against War and Fascism, and never belonged to it, and naturally would not sponsor it. It is true I did know Ambassador Dodd. I had called upon him at the time of the Hitler blood purge of June 30 and July 1, 1934. I would have been happy to have been present at any meeting that Ambassador Dodd addressed, but I did not, and I am saying this as definitely as I can, give my name as a sponsor to any such meeting, as far as I can recall.

I knew what the United Front was. In 1935, I was contributing a syndicated weekly article to newspapers in the Middle West. I had written one entitled "The United Front, A Menace," in which I had said:

Americans must not accept Communist leadership in order to avoid Fascist leadership.

Communists tell us that a Fascist dictatorship is inevitable in the United States. Hence they urge "The United Front" to combat war and fascism.

By that, they mean the union of socialists, liberals, pacifists, churchmen and progressives of every stripe, for the purpose of insuring peace and resisting fascism. Heretofore, these groups have never united. In fact, they have been convinced enemies of communism. Unfortunately, many liberals who fear fascism have been duped by the idea of the United Front. Its fundamental purpose is NOT to fight fascism.

Earl Browder, secretary of the Communist Party of the United States, has revealed its menacing objective. He writes, "The United Front is a method of struggle against the reformists, against the social-fascists, for the possession of the masses."

The official organ of the Communist Party of the United States, *The Communist*, in its January, 1935, issue stated, "The United Front is at the present time the main road along which the masses will be prepared for the struggle for Soviet power under the leadership of the Communist Party."

Intelligent Americans will denounce the proposal and seek to reveal its essential purpose. The Communist has no other purpose in the United Front program than to disrupt the American Federation of Labor and to insinuate himself into progressive movements in order to control them. Americans who are interested in maintaining the liberties of political democracy will repudiate the United Front.

Its real purpose is Divided Ranks. It is the "main road along which the masses will be prepared for the struggle." And the struggle, to use the Communist's own words, is "the violent overthrow of the whole existing capitalistic order, for the establishment of the proletariat."

The United Front is a dangerous Gift Horse.

One day, when I was president of DePauw University, a committee of five students waited upon me. I had had the closest relations with the students, and was surprised to find this little group with pads in hand and apparent agreement upon questions to be asked. When I started to answer, they started to scribble. I said, "What is the big idea? I want to talk to you. Why the note taking?" I noted the questions were catch questions, and I doubted very much the students had written them. This was my first experience with the American Student Union. I knew these students. One was the daughter of a noted

Methodist minister; one was subsequently to become an influential professor of philosophy. I made inquiry, and found that a Chapter of the American Student Union had been formed on the campus. I think it was finally composed of six or ten individuals. I was advised that one of the members was receiving a letter once a month from a New York source, which was thought to contain money. This little group insisted upon co-operating with the nation-wide student "peace strike" called for Armistice Day. I told them that we would do anything that was proper in the recognition of Armistice Day. We could have a great peace celebration, or any observance that the student body thought wise. This little group insisted upon a "student strike." I stated there was something fundamentally wrong here. A strike is usually a strike against something, not for something. I said, "I think somebody is trying to develop the strike technique in the American colleges for some purpose other than peace." I decided I would find out about this organization so I went to its headquarters in New York. It was a Communist headquarters, with three or four people working on some mailing lists. One of them wanted to know who I was. I told them. They appeared astonished, not to say perturbed. I asked for full information concerning the organization. I did not get it, but it was so apparent that this was a Communist setup that I went back determined that the American Student Union should have no influence upon the campus. I announced that any student who struck on Armistice Day would strike himself out, that is, he would be out of the University. At the Student Body's request, we brought Francis Lederer, the distinguished actor, to the campus. It was altogether a great Armistice celebration in which we honored the men who had died and in which we pledged ourselves to constructive efforts to develop a peaceful world. The Student Union did not strike. They held a little meeting of their own off the campus. Perhaps fifty or seventy-five students went over to hear what "the strikers" had to say. That was really the end of the American Student Union at DePauw University.

In August, 1953, a few weeks after the hearing, a young lady, now the wife of a doctor, called at our summer place at Lake Winnepesaukee. She was talking about the hearing. She said, "I resented it so deeply. Do you remember the American Student Union on our campus?" I answered, yes, I did. She continued, "I'll never forget the day you called the leaders of the student body to your office and you told them that this organization was Communist and that we would have nothing to do with it, and that if they struck they would find themselves off the campus for good. We couldn't believe it. We knew the students who were in the organization. We thought some of them were overdoing their peace emphasis, and we didn't think much of the strike, but I'll never forget how astounded I was when you told us that this was the penetration of communism into our campus. And to think that you should be up before a Committee when you had attitudes like that!"

Thus an individual who fought the United Front at its very inception, who had effectively blocked the infiltration of communism on the DePauw University campus, and who had clearly seen the purpose of the so-called "peace strike" has been publicized as being a sponsor of one of the major organizations of the United Front, namely, the American League Against War and Fascism, by a Congressional Committee too slovenly in research to get the facts, but all too ready to release falsehoods at public expense. The Committee had known for several years that I did not belong to this organization, but none the less clung to its false witness. A lie dies hard.

Mr. Kunzig seemed to be a little baffled by this answer, and asked, "Do you have any explanation or can you assist us by giving your viewpoint as to how your name could get into this sort of thing and how your name would be listed in *The Daily Worker* as one of the sponsors?"

I replied, as follows, "Yes, sir; I think I can. . . . Personally, I do not think too highly of the California Committee on Un-American

Activities, and hesitate to quote it, but on page 284 of the report of
the Tenney Committee of 1953, it declares:

"Communist-front organizations not only masquerade behind a respectable façade, endeavoring in all cases to conceal the real control and
objectives of the organizations by claiming to have some humanitarian
purpose, but they have also made use of the names of loyal individuals
without authority. From time to time, the Committee has received letters
of protest from persons who have been listed as officers of various front
organizations and who, in fact, have no connection whatever with these
movements, their names having been used without authority and for the
deliberate purpose of using non-Communist individuals as window-dress-
ing to divert suspicion. In such cases, the Committee is always eager and
willing to do everything in its power to correct this despicable practice."

Mr. Kunzig wanted to know whether I had sent a letter of protest.
He and his ilk create an atmosphere of conspiracy and insinuate
allegations designed to condemn. In 1953, facing the Communist
menace as we do, it is assumed that one in 1934 was first of all
aware of the fact that his name had appeared in *The Daily Worker*
as a sponsor of a certain meeting and that the matter was so serious
that he would immediately write a formal protest. As a matter of
fact, I never knew my name had appeared in that connection until
I saw it in one of the releases of the Committee. Mr. Clardy states
this is one of the great services of the Committee. How utterly
ridiculous! Its publication compounds the original falsehood.

The publications of this Committee, including the last one of
Senator Nelson S. Dilworth, are in large part but a repetition of
the stuff in Appendix IX which the Committee on Un-American
Activities itself has locked up because of its inaccuracies.

Then Mr. Clardy took off. He said, "We have a lot of sworn testimony to the effect that many good people have been placed on what
they call a 'sucker list' and that they use those names either by notification or otherwise, and it has just occurred to me, in view of your
statement, that your name got on one of those sucker lists."

This was a statement which I could answer in no other way than, "It seems to me that might well be so . . . they will do anything that tends to their ends."

Of course, the introduction of the term "sucker list" was to place me in that category. Mr. Velde piously suggested that the Committee thought I "would be interested in knowing that your name was used as a sponsor, and if it had not been brought out, you wouldn't know that your name was used as a sponsor."

Then Mr. Kunzig introduced a letterhead of the American League for Peace and Democracy, an organization to which I had never belonged. He introduced it by saying that it contains "a large list of leading Communists, such as Paul Robeson, Dorothy Parker, and others."

I had previously stated I had no association whatsoever with this organization, but he had an "exhibit" and introduced it. He turned abruptly and inquired whether when I had been a so-called editorial adviser of *The Protestant Digest* I had known that Louis Budenz, a former Communist, had testified concerning the *Digest*, alleging that the Communists had decided to make war on the Roman Catholic Church and that a comrade "advised him" the aim was to extend the work of *The Protestant* magazine. "That is the magazine whose name is 'Protestant' but which is engaged largely in being anti-Catholic, and the responsible Jewish organizations have recently condemned it, as you know."

Mr. Clardy interrupted at this place. This gray-haired gentleman, very wordy, stated, "Bishop Oxnam, this has troubled me as much, if not more, than all others that are in the files, because only recently we have had testimony, and I presided in the taking of that testimony, that will be released as soon as it is printed, which demonstrates clearly that that magazine was published as the result of a Communist directive and plot, that it was nefariously started, cleverly through using some good people, and I want you to know that, because in your answer and explanation I wish you would cover thoroughly your connection with it. It is most difficult for me to believe that you had any knowledge of that, and since that testimony has not been made public, I thought I should tell you about it in advance."

Here is an apparent gesture of kindness upon the part of a man who knew perfectly well that he was creating the conspiracy atmosphere and that it would be difficult for me to explain my relationship to a magazine he had already built up as a nefarious Communist plot. I replied, "I was an editorial adviser of *The Protestant*."

I continued, "First, you will please note that my relation to *The Protestant Digest* and to all the other organizations, and I say all— there are two or three that have been named—my relationship was prior to the time that they were declared subversive, and I had resigned from these two or three organizations prior to that time. I want that in the record."

Mr. Scherer broke in, and said, "Bishop, weren't they declared subversive because of the activities they engaged in during the time that you were connected with them?"

This is a very clever ruse, underhanded and undermining, and is in keeping with the ridiculous assertion of the counsel, namely, that when an agency is cited that citation is retroactive. It should be noted that the counsel does not indicate any of the activities which the Committee alleges were occurring at the time one was connected with an agency. As I stated in the case of the Committee of American-Soviet Friendship in Massachusetts, I know of no action whatsoever that was taken during that entire time that could be in any way declared to be subversive. This vicious declaration is tantamount to conviction. It insists that an individual who resigned from an organization long before it was declared subversive by the Attorney General was nevertheless engaged in activities, unspecified and unproved, alleged to have gone on. Mr. Scherer, a lawyer, draws the conclusion that an organization cited in 1953 was a conspiracy in 1943.

A striking example of the absurd assertion of Counsel Kunzig is seen in the case of the American Youth Congress which was infiltrated and did come under Communist control. Benjamin Gitlow, a former Communist, in his testimony before the House Committee on Un-American Activities actually stated that this organization was formed by Gene Tunney, James A. Farley and Herbert Hoover. If Mr. Kunzig is correct, then it means that these distinguished gentlemen were participating in subversive activity.

My answer was as follows: "When I received an invitation from the editor, whose name was Kenneth Leslie, a man whom I did not know and I think I have never met more than once or twice in my life, he invited me to go on the editorial board. He sent me a letter, and the names upon the editorial board were upon that letter.

"There were the names of Rev. Dr. George A. Buttrick, president of the Federal Council of Churches, one of the distinguished ministers of this nation; Dr. William Ernest Hocking, who then was a professor at Harvard University; Dr. Rufus M. Jones of the American Friends Service [Committee], one of the outstanding Quakers of this nation; Rev. Dr. Reinhold Niebuhr of the Union Theological Seminary, who is, I suppose, the outstanding theologian in the United States today. . . .

"That letterhead also carried this statement, *The Protestant Digest* wakens those of us who happen to be Protestants to a realization of our responsibilities and interests in the world.' That was signed by Eleanor Roosevelt. I asked Mr. Leslie in a letter that I wrote to him just what editorial advice meant, would it mean board meetings regularly? What would we be called upon to do?

"He replied that it would be as much or as little as we would want.

"I went into this, and I have forgotten when it was, 1940, was it— yes, in March of 1940.

"On February 11, 1942, I wrote this letter to Kenneth Leslie:

"I find that *The Protestant* is engaged in numerous activities related to national policy, legislation, and the like, and that statements go forth from the magazine to the public, quite apart from the magazine itself. Many gain the impression that such statements have the approval of your

Editorial Advisers. Several years ago, I decided not to serve on bodies unless I could give sufficient time to the formulation of policy to justify my name as a Board Member or Adviser. So far, there have been no meetings of the group associated with *The Protestant*, and the material that appears is never considered by this group. I think I must ask you to accept my resignation and to drop my name from the list of Editorial Advisers.

"I resigned. But why did I do that?"

MR. VELDE: "What was the date?"

BISHOP OXNAM: "February 11, 1942."

MR. VELDE: "How long were you an editorial adviser?"

BISHOP OXNAM: "I have stated that I was an editorial adviser from, I believe, March, 1940, to February, 1942. Please remember this was a monthly magazine, that for a time was published only once in two months. Now, why did I resign? Because Mr. Roger Baldwin of the American Civil Liberties Union one day came to me and said, 'Bishop, I wonder if you know who is really back of *The Protestant Digest*.'

"I said, 'What do you mean?'

"He said, 'I would look into it very carefully. I think that magazine has Communist support.'

"Mr. Roger Baldwin is a man who knew that whole field intimately. I resigned because of what he told me, after having looked into the matter.

"Interestingly enough, one of the most influential churchmen, Bishop Edwin Holt Hughes, who was formerly here in Washington, was an adviser. I called him and told him immediately upon receiving this information from Mr. Baldwin that he ought to get his name off that list. That is my relationship to the magazine."

MR. FRAZIER: "Did I understand you to say that you did resign as editor of this magazine prior to the time it had been declared a Communist-front organization?"

BISHOP OXNAM: "I was never an editor. I was on the board called the Advisory Board. The board never met, as a matter of fact. . . . I did resign in 1942. I think the Attorney General's list came out, if I recall correctly, in 1947."

It was at this point that Mr. Kunzig said, "I might add that the lists are retroactive."

I was determined not to allow the "anti-Catholic" label used by Louis Budenz to stick. I said, "Mr. Chairman, the second matter, which is the important matter, was the [alleged] anti-Catholicism of this magazine. I want to make this statement here for the record. Personally, I abhor religious division here. In an hour when faith is under attack around the world, there ought not to be religious division. I have been one who has been working for the reunion of the Christians of the world. It so happens that upon one or two issues I have had to take a stand and some have interpreted that as anti-Catholicism. I want the same liberties for every Roman Catholic that I want for every Protestant. I want the same liberties for the Roman Catholic Church that I want for the Protestant Church. We worship the same God. We adore the same Christ. We are inspired by the same Holy Spirit.

"Reference was made to this matter, and I want to say that there is no anti-Catholicism in my spirit whatsoever. There ought not to be religious division, and I think this may clear this matter, at least for the record. Please remember Mr. Louis Budenz was quoted in this matter." I picked up a booklet and said, "This comes from an address, the Episcopal Address I had the honor to read before the General Conference of the Methodist Church in 1948 and which was signed by the Bishops of the Methodist Church.

"Here is what I said, in part: 'The Protestant churches must continue the present brotherly and inspiring co-operation with the Eastern Orthodox Churches until such time as Protestantism is itself reunited. They may then consider union with Eastern Orthodoxy, which it is prayerfully hoped may be consummated. When the full union of Protestantism and of Eastern Orthodoxy is accomplished and the Christians of the world belong to but two great churches, the leadership of that day may be Christian enough and creative enough to kneel before a common altar, beg forgiveness of the Christ for disunity and, sharing in the bread and wine of Holy Communion, rise in His Spirit to form the Holy Catholic Church to which all Christians may belong.'

"I do not want anything in this record that would suggest anti-Catholicism in my spirit.

"I happen to be the only Protestant, I think, who has ever had the privilege of signing a statement with Cardinal O'Connell which we worked out together and was signed in Boston when there was anti-Semitism there and Jewish boys were being beaten in the streets. That happens to be my spirit, and when Mr. Budenz refers to that item, I would like to refer to this item."

Mr. Velde said, "In my opening statement, I mentioned, of course, that this is not to be construed by anyone as an investigation of religion or of religious freedoms in this country. I regret very much that you brought the subject of anti-Catholicism up at all."

I replied, "Mr. Chairman, it was brought up by your counsel, not by me."

Apparently, he did not hear, or if hearing, he paid no attention. He said, "As you know, eight out of nine members of this Committee are Protestants."

I then said, "I do not mean to be out of order, but your counsel raised that question, and I want to make it clear that there is no anti-Catholicism in my spirit, and what I am saying is precisely what you are saying."

The give and take of the record indicates that Mr. Kunzig wanted to get out of the matter as quickly as possible and that the chairman either did not know what was going on or, if he knew, was unwilling to face the implications of his own statement.

Mr. KUNZIG: "You stated, Bishop Oxnam, that you left this organization in February, 1942. Can you explain why your name is listed as an Editorial Adviser in August-September, 1942, as is shown on this Exhibit Number 13?"

BISHOP OXNAM: "No, I don't think it is necessary to explain it. I have the letter here and my recollection of the date of it. Whether my name appeared later has nothing to do with me, sir."

Mr. Kunzig referred to it as a "Communist magazine."

I said, "Just a moment, it was no Communist magazine, so far as I knew. In February 11, 1942, I resigned. You are showing me an issue of August-September, 1942. I did not even know there was an issue between February and this. I have heard that the magazine was published monthly through May of 1940, then bi-monthly, monthly again, and now quarterly. It has dwindled to a pamphlet size by now, and is begging for money. I don't know anything about it following February 11, 1942."

MR. JACKSON: "What was the date of the last exhibit?"

MR. KUNZIG: "August-September, 1942."

MR. DOYLE: "If it was Communist dominated, you would expect them to take advantage of the Bishop's name in the six months, wouldn't you?"

MR. VELDE: "Mr. Doyle, with all respect to you, we have asked all members to follow the written, the regular rules of procedure. So would you please address the chair?"

MR. DOYLE: "I will the next time. I thought there was a lull and recess in the meeting."

MR. VELDE: "Proceed, Mr. Kunzig."

Then Mr. Kunzig proceeded to introduce material that was taken in an executive session with Manning Johnson, a former member of the National Committee of the Communist Party, testifying on July 13. I doubt very much that Mr. Johnson can stand up under cross-examination anywhere.

Mr. Kunzig went on to read from this testimony until finally I had to break in by asking, "Might I ask, is the counsel testifying? I heard all this about *The Protestant*. What has it to do with me? I indicated when I resigned and why. And I do not quite understand this long recitation of a witness of a day or two ago."

Mr. Jackson broke in again with Mr. Scherer's thesis, "The fact is that the activity of the publication which led to its citation was going on at the time you were an editorial adviser. I do not say that you contributed to it in any way. However, I think that it is relevant and material and cannot be deleted."

I referred again to my opposition to the United Front. Mr. Velde broke in, saying, "You are getting out of line, Bishop, and I would like to have you answer the question as nearly as possible."

Mr. Velde allowed members of the Committee to travel over the earth. He allowed his counsel to go on and on, repeating material that had been testified to by a witness whose reputation is under serious question. Mr. Clardy then broke in, stating, "It seems to me that, in view of the fact that you have continually attacked all investigating committees, including this one . . ." This was false, and Mr. Clardy knew it. He affirmed that the magazine known as *The Protestant* "was Communist in origin and inception and in practice in ways that perhaps even you did not see." His conclusion was I ought to be appreciative, therefore, of the work of the Committee. Now here were two lies in a single paragraph. I had not attacked all investigating committees. I attacked the procedures of this one. There are some investigating committees that have rendered excellent service. I do not think it has been proved at all that *The Protestant* magazine was in origin and inception Communist. Then, of course, it all comes out. Mr. Clardy had spoken, as he says for thirty seconds on February 25, in response to an address that I had delivered at the American University. He said, "You did not know me. You had never heard of me. I had heard briefly of you, but I really knew nothing of you. It was an implication of criticism by association because I had been made a member of the Committee which had not acted and with which I had nothing to do up to that point, which had not even had a hearing because at that time it made it very plain and very clear, to me at least, that you were through this method . . ."

Mr. Velde broke in, and said, "Are you asking a question, Mr. Clardy?"

MR. CLARDY: "I will. I am building up to it. I want to ask him something very personal on it, and it is a matter of personal privilege more or less, because it troubles me. The question is this, when you made that speech and then we exchanged brief communication, why did you not exhibit the spirit of charity that I think all of us should have and frankly admit that you did not intend to include me or Mr. Scherer in the blanket indictment which you delivered against the entire Committee on which we had just been appointed?"

Mr. Velde expressed the hope we could conclude the matter today and that we should not pursue personalities further. Mr. Clardy bowed to the ruling of the chair. Of course, Mr. Clardy knew perfectly well what he was saying was not in accord with fact. I had criticized the Committee in this connection because of an action of its present chairman in the present Administration. It was the action in which he had attacked Mrs. Agnes E. Meyer. Mr. Clardy knew that. He was a member of the Committee. Once again, if this Committee were really interested in *The Protestant* magazine, if it had reason to believe that *The Protestant* magazine was subversive, why did it fail to advise the men who were acting as editorial advisers of its information, or to have conferred with them individually? But no, the matter is released before checking, with no statement to the effect that the individual resigned from the editorial board the moment that he had reason to believe there was anything irregular in its activities.

The next question involved another magazine. Mr. Kunzig asked, "Sir, did you ever contribute to a magazine or publication entitled *Soviet Russia Today?*" The "investigators" did not have a copy of the article in question and therefore had not read it. This attack began with a flourish of trumpets and the roll of the citation drum.

Mr. Kunzig announced that this magazine was cited by a Special Committee of the House Un-American Activities in 1944, cited in a report issued in 1942, which he announced was prior to the time I contributed the article. What does this mean? Is an American citizen required to read all of the voluminous material published by this Committee, including the 2,166 pages of Appendix IX which the Committee itself now repudiates? Mr. Kunzig went on to cite a report of the Committee issued in 1953, and of the California Committee of 1948 and the Massachusetts Committee of 1938. He did not tell his audience that a report appearing in one state is copied by the investigators of another state. There was no indication of the fact that citations do not mean careful investigation.

The discarded Appendix IX lists me as belonging to the American Round Table on India. It also lists Governor Thomas E. Dewey among the suspect. I had never heard of the American Round Table on India until I saw it listed in Chapter X of John T. Flynn's widely circulated book entitled *The Road Ahead*. I checked and found that this allegation had been reprinted in numerous reports by self-appointed sleuthing or superpatriotic organizations. The listing of a lie in a report by a State Committee on Un-American Activities or by the Committee on Un-American Activities of the House of Representatives is printed and reprinted, without investigation, by such private agencies. Further inquiry elicited the information that this organization was set up by a wealthy gentleman who lives at the Waldorf-Astoria Hotel in New York. I was advised that the purpose had been to call upon India and England to mediate their differences and that the organization tapered off in about a year when it appeared that the two countries would mediate. It appears that all the committee ever did was to meet in this gentleman's office, with numerous telephones that were upon his desk ringing throughout the session, and concoct letters for the press on this subject. Whenever this item appears in a list of agencies I am alleged to have belonged to, it is alleged that a Robert K. Norton referred to as "a well-known Communist," was also a member of the group. Such listings are called citations.

The shoddiness that characterizes such "investigation" would not be tolerated in business. They confused this Round Table with the International Round Table, over which I had presided at the Princeton Inn, and which was attended by responsible church leaders from many countries, among them John Foster Dulles, Henry P. Van Dusen and Roswell P. Barnes.

It was a galling and degrading experience to sit through such questions. I knew that any American could be caught up in this web of "citation" and destroyed. There were moments when I looked up at some of these Committeemen and found it difficult to maintain composure. I knew what they were trying to do. It was hard to bank the fires of inner resentment and to keep them from blazing up in undignified speech. I recalled that Mr. Kunzig himself had told me that he had never seen Appendix IX. This meant that the attorney for the Committee had failed to trace the allegations to their sources. Actually Appendix IX was originally published in seven volumes. Its purpose was to preserve the files of the Dies Committee which at the time, it was believed, were threatened with destruction. Seven thousand sets, which cost twenty thousand dollars to publish, were delivered to the Committee. Benjamin Mandell, a chief investigator for the Committee at one time, declared the exhibits in Appendix IX are "a fair cross section of our files today." But when Appendix IX was brought to the attention of the full Committee, it was ordered restricted and existing copies destroyed. Many sets had already been sold. I myself studied Appendix IX in one of the libraries of Washington. It is inaccessible in the Congressional Library, having been impounded by the Committee. These volumes are entitled *Communist Front Organizations with Special Reference to the National Citizens Political Action Committee.* The names of so many distinguished citizens were included in these malicious and misleading reports that it is no wonder the

Committee ordered copies destroyed. Unfortunately, these copies are today used by intelligence officers and private individuals and form the base of much unfounded accusation.

There is no opportunity to present a case when an individual appears before a Committee as I did. If I had been given an hour to point out the falsehoods in my so-called "file" or had had opportunity to question the Counsel or the research staff, I could have presented the material which would have convinced any fair Committee. This is not the procedure. The accuser becomes the accused and must defend himself. I knew this as Mr. Kunzig pressed his question concerning *Soviet Russia Today*. I informed the Committee that I had been requested to write an article and had done so. The article was entitled "A Churchman Evaluates Yalta." I informed the Committee that editorial changes had been made without my consent and that a request for a subsequent article had been rejected because I had resented unauthorized editorial changes which had eliminated certain critical statements.

The Committee had neither studied the article nor seen the April, 1945, number in which it had appeared. That issue carries a cover picture of a young Russian sailor with a boyish smile. After the page announcing the contents is a full-page photograph carrying the caption "The Big Three Leading the Great Allied Drive to Berlin and Victory." On the upper left is a photograph of Field Marshal Sir Bernard L. Montgomery, commanding ground assault forces. On the right is Marshal Gregory K. Zhugov, the Red Army Chief of Staff and Deputy to Marshal Stalin, commanding First Byelo-Russian Army. In the center—this is the wording of the caption—"Our Own General Dwight D. Eisenhower, Supreme Allied Commander in the West." The next three pages are review and comment; they deal with the Yalta Conference and President Roosevelt's appeal to the people, the Anti-Crimea Camp, the World Trade Union Congress, the sixteen correspondents who attacked William L. White's book on Russia, and recount the International Woman's Day celebration whose guests of honor were Mrs. Eleanor Roosevelt, Madame Andrei Gromyko, wife of the Soviet Ambassador to the United States, Madame Wei Tao-Ming, wife of the Chinese Ambassador, Madame Honore Bonnet, wife of the French Ambassador, and Lady Katherine Sansom, wife of the British Minister for Far Eastern Affairs, representing Lady Halifax. There was additional comment relative to a young Russian general who had been killed and to Alexei Tolstoy, a writer, as well as a section dealing with support for Russian war relief. Then follows an article entitled "A Churchman Evaluates Yalta." It is less than a page in length. At the bottom is a picture of Churchill, Roosevelt and Stalin.

Why it should be considered subversive to have contributed an article upon the Yalta Conference to this magazine, I do not know. The purpose of *Soviet Russia Today* was alleged to be the stimulation of better relations between the United States and Russia. There were articles by Russian governmental representatives, as well as an article by a representative of our own Department of Commerce. Was the purpose in introducing my article at the hearing any other than to raise question concerning my loyalty?

Mr. Kunzig did not explain how an article appearing in a magazine at the time the United States and Russia were allies and were fighting for our existence was subversive. Had he known it, he might have asked why I was in Germany at the time the American Armed Forces joined up with the Russian Army at Torgau. I was there upon invitational orders of the Joint Chiefs of Staff and carried a letter from President Franklin D. Roosevelt. Mr. Kunzig could have left that out and have asked, "Is it true that you were with the American armies at such a moment?" I personally did not meet the Russians, but I remember vividly the dinner hour with our officers who had been with the Russians through the day. The Russians wanted their eagles, maple leaves and bars for souvenirs, and had given their own insignia in exchange. It was a boisterous evening, and all were in jocular mood. The war was coming to an end. Is the fact that I was with the Armed Forces at that particular time going to be held up some day as evidence of Soviet sympathy?

Throughout the day Mr. Velde ruled with an iron hand. The Democratic minority was treated with scant courtesy. Mr. Doyle referring to *Soviet Russia Today* had interjected, "There are others among the contributors. There is a United States Senator listed here, for instance—two of them. There are two of them listed as recent contributors, and other well-known names to the American public."

Mr. Velde replied sarcastically, "Does the gentleman want to investigate or to—"

Mr. Doyle answered, "No, I do not want to investigate."

Mr. Velde shut him off with, "I think with all due respect to you, Mr. Doyle, we are getting out of the realm of this investigation."

Mr. Doyle's rejoinder was pertinent, "I do not think it is out of the realm of the investigation to show the actual fact. We are only naming one person as a recent contributor, and there are a dozen or two dozen in the same magazine. That is the purport of my question. I just wanted the record to show that there are other distinguished Americans who are also contributors to that book. I think it is very pertinent and very material to this question of the Bishop."

Discussion followed and Mr. Velde again expressed the hope we might finish the hearing today. In order to finish today, he hoped we might confine our questions and answers to the subject matter under discussion. I interjected, "Mr. Chairman, if we could deal with some of the errors that I have tried to point out, we could perhaps clear the record. I realize what is being done here, and I am trying to answer, sir, responsively, but I particularly referred to errors in the record which I think could be cleared if I were questioned upon them."

Mr. Kunzig ignored the request and turned to the National Federation for Constitutional Liberties. This was an organization with which I had no association whatsover. He then asked, "Did you have any knowledge that the Marshall Foundation, which is a cited fund, a Communist cited fund, gave $65,000 to this group and was a large financial backer to this organization?"

I replied, "Since I was not a member of it and had no relationship with it, I had no knowledge concerning this until you state it."

Of course, all of this was introduced into the record for but a single purpose. He stated that my name appeared in two messages sent out by this organization. I have since looked up these messages and find that in one case my name is spelled incorrectly, and in the other, I am referred to as Rev. G. Bromley Oxnam. Usually when my name has appeared on a public petition the name is put as Bishop G. Bromley Oxnam. It suggests that somebody else had signed my name. In any case, I said, "I have tried to say that I had no relationship that I recall at all with that organization."

◀ V ▶

I protest against the un-American assumption that underlies many utterances of these Committeemen, namely, that accusation constitutes conviction. The uncorroborated identification of a citizen as a Communist by an unknown informer is not proof, and the publication of the names of persons thus identified is a vicious and un-American practice.

IT WAS at this point that Mr. Velde tried again to justify the Committee, asking, "Bishop, may I ask you, when did you first learn that your name was used in this connection?"

I replied, "Several of these I knew nothing about, sir, until I saw the releases of this Committee."

Thinking he saw an opening in the line, Mr. Velde tried to

plunge through. An experienced backfield man would know better. He said, "Again I want to say and I hope you appreciate the fact that this Committee has done some service in releasing those files, because you like any other American citizen would be interested in whether your name was used in connection with Communist-front organizations. I am sure you appreciate that."

I most emphatically disagree. To release in public a citizen's name in this fashion is in no sense to help him. It is really to harm him. I said in reply, "Mr. Chairman, if that information were sent to me, it would be of service, but when that information is broadcast, and it is assumed that I belong to organizations I did not belong to, that is the disservice that I am requesting the Committee to end as far as I am concerned."

Mr. Kunzig was clever enough to know that direct answers of this sort undermined his case. He tried to move away quickly, and said, "For the record I should like to incorporate into the record, and to be brief, the Communist background, the cited background of this organization—"

I interrupted him saying, "Mr. Chairman, why should that be in? Is that pertinent when I have said I do not belong to it? Why does he insert in my record a whole Communist relationship to an organization I do not belong to?"

Mr. Velde backed up his counsel, saying, "Because we want to get the record straight. We have your denial of belonging to the organization, and this will be inserted in the record as your denial of belonging to the organization so that we finally may get your record straight so that we may inform the American people regarding their activities, what you did belong to and what you did not belong to." Actually, the files could have been cleared in a day. The Committee had failed to get "the record straight."

Mr. Velde's utterances were at times involved, a little hard to understand. What it added up to was this. When you stated you did not belong to an organization, the Committee deliberately put in the alleged conspiratorial record of that organization in its entirety. It thus appears in my record, and it will be quite easy for someone to say, "The Committee asked the Bishop whether he belonged to the National Federation for Constitutional Liberties. The Bishop, of course, denied it, but we should have in mind what that organization really is." Is the purpose to investigate, to make clear, or to intimidate? My objection to this method was overruled.

Mr. Kunzig then made reference to the Medical Bureau and North American Committee to Aid Spanish Democracy. He wanted to know if I had been a national sponsor of the organization.

I replied, "Mr. Chairman, I have explained that when the Spanish people sought the freedom that we possess, I was in complete sympathy with the endeavor. . . . Several committees were organized to aid them, just as at present I am a member of Congressman Judd's Committee to Aid the Intellectuals in China. [This is an organization to help intellectual escapees from Red China's tyranny.] If some Chinese should some day be proved to be a Communist who has been aided by Congressman Judd's committee, I suppose some committee 20 years from now might be having somebody up asking about that.

"Now, in this matter there was an interfaith division of what was called the American Committee for Spanish Freedom. I did belong to that. I despised Franco and that entire regime just as I did Stalin and do the regime in Russia today."

I did not know the Pope would soon confer the Order of Christ, one of Rome's highest decorations, upon the dictator who was an ally of Hitler and indirectly responsible for the death of American soldiers. I went on to say, "In the matter of sending medical aid to these people, I have no apology for that whatsover. I did belong, and I find that other individuals such as Norman Vincent Peale—Dr. Peale was a member of the same committee. We thought we were in a good humanitarian organization and were doing our best to help what we thought to be a worthy cause."

Mr. Kunzig said, "I think the record must show clearly, and to have the record clear, I wish to incorporate, Mr. Chairman, the fact that this American Committee for Spanish Freedom was cited as Communist by the Attorney General in 1949."

I asked, "Mr. Chairman, ought there not to be in the record when I belonged to it?

Mr. Kunzig answered, "Yes. Let us put completely in the record when you belonged to it, sir. It was January 21, 1946, the period for which activities of this group were cited as subversive." That was the terminal date and Mr. Kunzig knew it. He put on the same record that had been used throughout the day and proved himself to be a competent disk jockey.

In such a hearing, a counsel has a case to make. His job depends upon his ability to save the face of the Committee. He resorts to clever devices and while admitting that an organization had not been declared subversive by the Attorney General at the time under discussion, he insists that the activities which occasioned such later citation were going on when an individual is alleged to have been related to the organization. There is no introduction of fact. What subversive activities were going on? Who participated in them? It is impossible to answer a blanket charge. It is true that Communists did infiltrate some worthy organizations. It is true that they set up organizations and did secure the co-operation of patriotic Americans. It was difficult to distinguish between the worthy and the unworthy organizations. Without having produced a single fact to justify the allegation of subversive activities upon the part of an agency that sought to render medical aid to men who were struggling for freedom, Mr. Velde said, "Bishop, I am just a little bit puzzled at how you could belong to such an organization, having stated that you had been anti-Communist all your life, and not realize that the Communist Party was infiltrating these particular organizations. Can you explain that?"

Once again, the time factor was ignored. There was a considerable period before the Communists and the Nazis moved into the Spanish struggle. I explained to Mr. Velde that these organizations were set up to achieve a worthy purpose. Sponsorship did not mean attending regular meetings and sitting in on the formulation of policy. As a matter of fact, I never attended any meeting of the interfaith division of the American Committee for Spanish Freedom. It was headed by a gentleman in whom I had complete confidence, Bishop Lewis O. Hartman.

I told Mr. Velde that I belonged to a number of organizations at the present time, for instance, the organization that General Carl Spaatz had set up whose purpose was to help people who are today living in tyranny behind the Iron Curtain. I said that we were in danger of refusing to belong to any voluntary organization. Americans have always sought worthy ends by setting up organizations to secure support, both financial and personal, and I added, "Perhaps we ought to come to the place where you lend your name to nothing. I think as a matter of fact we are in danger of getting right to that place." Sponsorship is presented as participation in secret association with conspirators. Referring to the Committee, I raised a question as to whether the Committee itself had the names of the real conspirators. "I do not know whether the Rosenbergs or whether the rest of that group were known to the Committee. . . . But I have sometimes wondered if we are not spending so much time in this guilt-by-association business that we are not getting at the fundamental matter. Some of us would like to help upon that, and as I said a little earlier, sir, this whole question of causes—I wish there were opportunity in a committee like this to deal with Asia as I think I know it and to make some suggestions to remove the causes."

These Committee members with the knowledge of 1953 talked as though they were fully acquainted with all of these matters back for thirty years. The truth is they were not. The information was not available. The climate was of different nature. These cloak-and-dagger boys swagger up and down the halls of Congress giving the impression that they have saved the nation from Communist revolution. If the entire record of this Committee is added up, the number of persons that they have discovered who are really a danger to their country is so small as to raise serious questions as to what the Committee itself has been doing.

The Committee tried to trip me up and to put the phrase "lend one's name" in the worst possible light. Mr. Jackson asked, "Don't you think that the use of those names by these organizations did in fact bring into the groups a great many Americans who might otherwise never have been associated with the group except by the fact that prominent names did appear?"

I replied, "When one lends his name to an organization, if the name is of strength he may be giving some strength to the organization. He lends his name, however, not to an organization that is a conspiracy in his knowledge, and I don't think the inference should be drawn later that he did that thing."

I pointed out that this was precisely what the Committee itself was doing. It was lending its name to libel when it released material that was false and sought to avoid responsibility by stating later that it did not vouch for the accuracy of the material.

Mr. Velde broke in and insisted that the material that was released was known to the public. He said, "Bishop, it wasn't the Committee that released it. It had been in the newspapers and was public information."

This was something I had hoped he would say, and I replied immediately, "Mr. Chairman, I am so glad you put that here. An announcement in a newspaper has only the strength of the announcement, but when the Committee on Un-American Activities, a committee of the United States Congress, takes up a newspaper report and includes it in a file, it has an entirely different standing, and the Committee, I think, by releasing on its official letterheads is doing the very thing that Mr. Jackson is accusing some of us who may have lent our names, because sending out this information is damaging, and particularly when it isn't true."

The Committee had released numerous false statements to the

effect that I had sponsored organizations with which I had no association whatsoever. I continued, "Now, I think Mr. Jackson is right, when you lend your name you do give certain influence, and when the Committee lends its name in certain statements concerning me it is doing precisely the same thing, and that is why I am here asking this record to be cleared."

Mr. Velde replied, "We will co-operate in every way in clearing the record and that is the purpose of this hearing."

"Thank you, sir," I said.

The loose thinking that characterizes a good deal of the questioning was revealed in Mr. Walter's question. "Then don't you think that you were, to say the least, very careless in permitting your name to be used by anybody that saw fit to be using it?"

"I have not allowed my name to be used by anybody that saw fit," I replied. "If you will list all that has been brought in here—you have a handful of organizations, and I think I have shown in some cases, I believe, these organizations were worthy organizations. I don't lend my name loosely, and I don't think this Committee would like to feel it was lending the Committee prestige loosely to the circulation of information concerning me. It is the same thing."

Mr. Jackson sought to reduce the force of my statement that the name of Dr. Norman Vincent Peale had appeared upon the Interfaith Division of the American Committee for Spanish Freedom. He said, "I don't know whether he appeared on other letterheads or documents of organizations or not, but I would be inclined to think probably they were few in number." He then repeated the falsehood that he had sent out over his own signature again and again. Referring to me, he said, "In this instance they are not few in number. It forms a considerable amount of documentation."

A documented lie is still a lie. A dupe accepts a false document as truth. I said to Mr. Jackson, "One of the proposals I made to this Committee had to do with the release of such items before an individual was consulted to find out whether or no the material were true. Now, there is the fundamental issue. If, for instance, you receive information and then with an investigative setup such as this Committee must possess fail to come even 300 yards to an office to ask whether or no this is true and you still release it, that to me is the question, and it would seem to me there ought to be some procedure whereby we do not release material concerning an individual that is unverified, for which the Committee assumes no responsibility . . ."

Mr. Velde struggled to back the Committee rather than to search for the truth. I had referred to one of the items released in the Committee files, namely, that I had written an article upon Stalin. I had not written the article. Mr. Velde apparently could not get it through his head. He said, "Certainly, Bishop, that is not the fault of the Committee. You must blame that on someone else besides the Committee if the story went out that was adverse to you and quoted some of the material in the public files. The Committee, as I said before, only assembles this information which has been made public a long time ago."

When an article written by someone else is attributed to me, the fact that the article written by somebody else appeared in public does not justify the Committee in its announcement that I had written it. Mr. Velde's response was amazing. He said, "That was an occurrence that happened during the 82nd Congress."

Thus, the Committee goes back thirty years to dig up derogatory material to condemn, but assumes no responsibility for its own activities prior to January, 1953.

Apparently, the Committee was unwilling to give up its "lend your name" refrain. Mr. Clardy said, "Don't you think that anyone who occupies a position in connection with education, or a clergyman, does, as Mr. Walter has suggested, occupy a special position that calls for a special care in these troubled days in joining any organization, since the Communists have spread their conspiracy so far? Don't you think that this Committee, therefore, is doing a good job in letting all of you know who these organizations are and how the Communists operate?" Throughout the day, Mr. Clardy had tried to get some admission which would be an indirect approval of procedures that I regard as un-American.

I replied, "Mr. Clardy, when this Committee published a volume called *Communism in Action* [which was prepared by a competent scholar, the Director of the Legislative Reference Service of the Library of Congress, Dr. Ernest S. Griffith] it did an excellent job." I then pointed out that an individual who would lower himself by using the methods of the research staff of the House Committee could take the factual description of religion in Russia that appeared in the Committee's own volume entitled *Communism in Action,* and by quoting statement after statement show that the Committee was really guilty of Communist sympathies. Any factual statement that appears favorable, or contradicts the hysterical reporting of some irresponsibles, is suspect. I stated Dr. Griffith's report "was a correct description of what was going on," and added, "That is what we need. We need the facts." I added, "When we have the releases, however, that are not factual, that begins to involve a man's personal liberty, and that is the issue I am after here."

Mr. Doyle seized the opportunity to say, "This has apparently been about a fifteen-minute period of observations. I just wish to make the observation, therefore, that I think the members of the Committee, my colleagues, have manifested much wisdom in these last few minutes with the Bishop, and I think the Bishop also has given the benefit of much wisdom and suggestions to the Committee. I would be less than true to myself if I didn't say that I think the Bishop has given us something to think about, as well as I think we have given him something to think about."

Mr. Kunzig never wanted a favorable comment to lodge itself in the public mind, so he turned to the National Committee to Abolish the Poll Tax. He said that my name was listed as one of its sponsors. I replied, "I don't know anything about this organization. I would like to see the poll tax abolished, as a matter of fact. That is an opinion that has no relevance here, but I don't know anything about this organization." He had handed me the document, and I said, "I do see the name of a lady I know, Mary McLeod Bethune, a great Negro leader. . . .

"I would have to answer, to the best of my recollection, I have no knowledge concerning this, although I do see the name of the Right Rev. Henry W. Hobson, the Episcopal Bishop of Southern Ohio, here, and if I had time—I see here another one, Fiorello H. La-Guardia. And I am interested in this, sir; I find the name of the Most Rev. Robert E. Lucey, of the Roman Catholic Church, in this list."

Robert E. Lucey is an archbishop. "I must say this is a pretty good list," I continued. "Here is Mrs. J. D. Bragg, who is the head of the Women's Organization of the Methodist Church." I went on to say that to my recollection I had never seen this before, but I would not be likely to be thought in bad company in the light of some of the names that I have read there. "I must say I don't recall it, sir, and that is the best answer I can give."

Here we have the mind-set of the Committee coming in again. Mr. Scherer said, "It is a communist organization; that is obvious, isn't it?"

I replied, "I don't know that this is a Communist organization. All I am told is by counsel, that this has been cited." I added, "It would seem to me if there could be some method whereby these organizations could be heard, and in the American way they could present their testimony to a committee of this kind, then if they say they are cited, well and good, but the Attorney General's list, I think, wasn't made up on the basis of hearings, was it?"

Mr. Kunzig, embarrassed by the fact I had read such distinguished names as Fiorello H. LaGuardia, stated that the names of Julius Emspak and Donald Ogden Stewart, alleged Communists, were included. He said, "Let's keep the record straight."

I replied, "I only read the names I knew there, and I didn't read all of them as a matter of fact."

The audience roared, and Mr. Velde said, "May I say to the audience again that if another demonstration like that takes place, either of approval or disapproval, I shall ask the Sergeant-at-Arms and the members of the Capitol Police Force to escort anyone who makes such an indication of approval or disapproval out of the hearing room."

◀ VI ▶

I protest against the "Big Bully" spirit and the bad manners of some Committeemen who lecture and berate a witness, and who through insinuation misrepresent the views and activities of the witness as well as secure head-lines for themselves in the press. A witness is forced to listen to the homilies of the ignoramus, the misrepresentation of the unscrupulous, and the brow-beating of the bully. I protest against such degrading and un-American procedures.

UPON two occasions the Committee was summoned to the House. During the recess, I was surrounded by journalists and others who asked questions. I sought to converse with Mr. Parlin who gave me a warning signal and pointed to a man who had taken his place immediately behind another person but within range of our voices. He carried a recording device which he sought to shield from view. It appeared wise to converse with no one, so I sat down and began to turn some of the pages of a file.

I recalled the debate with Mr. Jackson in which that very question had been raised. What is a file? I had demanded this hearing so that false and misleading allegations might be stricken from the file. The fact that this Committee was keeping files on more than a million Americans suggested the names of Himmler and of Beria. There was something un-American, it seemed to me, in the development of police state dossiers. I felt a certain degree of sympathy for the Committeemen who were dependent upon the information the research staff placed upon their desks. Unless these files were maintained with strict insistence upon accuracy, they may well mislead even sincere Committeemen, and their release to the public may destroy reputation and reduce the earning power of a citizen.

A person suffering from bubonic plague should be quarantined. But he must have the plague. What would we think of a health department that would put quarantine signs upon an American home because some malicious gossip declared she had heard that somebody said the accused had been with somebody who was alleged to have had the plague. The accusations released by this Committee are as damaging to reputation as quarantine signs would be to a business. What would happen to a restaurant if an irresponsible health official, without so much as a medical examination, were to put up a sign in front of a restaurant reading "BUBONIC PLAGUE" because he heard that one of the waitresses was ill. Patrons would, of course, shun the place. A health department must not be party to a lie. Many citizens believe, and understandably so, that a Congressional committee would not placard an individual without investigation. But that is precisely what this Committee has done and does. It admits it. It seeks to ameliorate the situation at present by announcing that it does not vouch for the truth of the quarantine sign. That is the "fine-type" aspect of this inexcusable practice.

This Committee published the testimony given in the secret hearings of early July, 1953. Before the accused were heard or even notified they had been accused, this Committee released the uncorroborated testimony of witnesses who were not cross examined and who were not called upon to confront the citizens they accused. This testimony cast suspicion upon three great religious leaders, two of whom are dead. The nation has possessed no more distinguished and devoted religious leaders than Dr. John Haynes Holmes, Rabbi Stephen S. Wise and Rabbi Judah L. Magnes. But this Committee rushes into print, and the patriotism of "six hundred" Protestant clergymen is questioned and even the dead are maligned. Rabbi Wise was a patriot and a great humanitarian, the friend and adviser of American Presidents, a man internationally known and respected, a religious leader loved by Christian and Jew alike. But in death, a committee permits practices that would blacken his name. No wonder the Jewish and Christian community spoke out in national protest. Would that the practices of this Committee might be subjected to the devastating logic of Rabbi Wise's towering intellect, and the nation once again hear his courageous and prophetic voice, and feel again the power of his personality. It is such as he who will save us from the practices that threaten the free way of life.

I wondered during the recess whether there would be some way to introduce into the record the material that this Committee had released concerning the National Council of Churches. It was apparent that it would have to be introduced in answering some other question. I did not like this oblique approach. It proved impossible to get the material in. I knew that the Committee had released a statement concerning the National Council which began with the astounding admission, "The Committee on Un-American Activities has never investigated the National Council of the Churches of Christ in the United States of America, nor has it made any finding concerning the activities of the group. However, public records, files and publications of this Committee contain the following information." Then followed twenty-one pages of so-called information relative to some of the most distinguished religious leaders of the United States. Who sent this material to the Committee? That it was released is clear since large sections of it appeared in a periodical representing an agency that publicly boasted it had "channeled" information concerning such religious leaders to the Committee on Un-American Activities.

Congressman Jackson had sought to define a file. He said, "A file is based upon the frequent and common occurrence of an individual's name in Communist fronts, his listing as a sponsor, director, editor, or contributor to Communist front or Communist publications, or the editorial comments of the activities of any given individual; consistent and favorable mention in Communist Party or Communist front publications; his personal actions which are intended to be divisive of the American people; the personal advocacy of the socialist state is certainly contributory to any file; a consistent advocacy of any part of all of the Soviet system; his opposition to any form of investigation of the Communist conspiracy or those who comprise it; his opposition to deportation of Communist Party members or alien Communist front members; his opposition to legislation designed to curb Communism; his opposition to the affirmation of loyalty (loyalty oaths); and his opposition to any form of military training. All of these factors are considered by the Committee. In addition, the use of such phrases as 'red baiting' and 'witch hunt' to describe the activities of the duly-constituted committees of the United States Congress is indicative of the Communist Party line. One who consistently deplores the suggestion of guilt by association, but who attempts to prove his own innocence by association is in a manner suspect."

As I recalled Mr. Jackson's statement, I remembered a pointed utterance of Edward A. Steiner. He said, "Ideas die of solitary confinement in some heads." Did Mr. Jackson understand what he had said? Among the categories which constitute the basis for a file, he had listed, "his opposition to any form of military training." Does this mean there is a file on Archbishop Cushing of Boston whose

opposition to compulsory military training is well known? Is Mr.
Jackson casting suspicion upon nearly all of the Protestant churches of
the United States, including "the little white church across the street
from my birthplace in South Dakota"? He had said in a Congressional speech, "I am a Congregationalist by birth and breeding." He
alleged that this little church held "a special place in my affection."
He became ecstatic and said, "But I see no threat to it and its counter-
parts throughout the great land in the words and actions of Harold
Velde. To the contrary, I feel that no greater service can be rendered
to God and man alike than to find out what men, if any, would place
the thorny crown of the Kremlin upon the brow of the Prince of
Peace." Did he know that the Congregational Church and nearly all
of the Protestant churches are on record officially in opposition to
compulsory military training? Are they replacing the Cross with the
Hammer and Sickle? It is not because these churches are opposed to
strong national defense that they have taken this action, but because
they doubt that compulsory military training is a significant contribution to national defense. They fear that militarization of our national
life. Mr. Jackson informs us that "the personal advocacy of the socialist state is certainly contributory to any file." Has Norman Thomas
suddenly become suspect? Since Mr. Jackson was reading from a prepared manuscript, his categories represent his thought. He says "that
opposition to any form of investigation of the communist conspiracy"
is a basis for a file. This is sheer totalitarianism. He says "any form
of investigation." He goes further and says "opposition to legislation
designed to curb communism." Does this mean that poorly considered
legislation, or dangerous legislation, is not to be opposed? What has
become of the democratic process? If a person uses such phrases as
"red baiting" and "witch hunt," the phrases must be considered as
"indicative of the Communist Party line." Does this mean that a file
must be kept upon Justice William O. Douglas who has used such
phrases? Is opposition to the bill proposed by Congressman Velde
to be regarded as justification for a file? He had seriously proposed

that the nine million volumes of the Congressional Library must be read and subversive passages indicated.

What is a file? It is really a collection of miscellaneous clippings, letterheads, dodgers, leaflets, which appear to indicate that an individual has been mentioned by, or co-operated with, allegedly subversive groups. This miscellanous material is selected by people either too incompetent to conduct research essential to ascertaining the views and activities of an individual or employed for the purpose of slanted selection designed to misrepresent. These public files do not represent investigation. They are a scissors and paste procedure in which incompetents clip items and fellow incompetents file them. It is this material that is released to the public. It is upon the basis of such material that a hearing such as mine was held.

During the recess, I wondered how I could call attention to the studies of the Committee that had been made by competent scholars. I knew that the activities of the Committee had not been subjected to careful appraisal by the general public. Most of the discussion had been heated and partisan, either for or against the Committee. The Communist threat was too serious to tolerate incompetent practices upon the part of such Committees, and in the mood of the moment, I realized anew that the rights of citizens are too precious to tolerate invasion upon the part of some who have sought to capitalize upon contemporary hysteria for politica' advantage.

Two significant studies are available, one by Father August Raymond Ogden entitled *The Dies Committee, A Study of the Special House Committee for the Investigation of Un-American Activities, 1938-1944,* published by the Catholic University of America Press in Washington, D.C. Father Ogden's carefully documented study concludes with the words, "This study of the Special House Committee for the Investigation of the Un-American Activities indicates that the said Committee was neither an ideal nor a desired means of exposing subversive activities."

Father Ogden reports that on August 12, 1938, Mr. Dies in support of the bill to establish the Committee had said,

It is easy to "smear" someone's name or reputation by unsupported charges or an unjustified attack, but it is difficult to repair the damage that has been done. . . .

In investigating un-American activities, it must be borne in mind that because we do not agree with the opinions or philosophies of others does not necessarily make such opinions or philosophies un-American. The most common practice engaged in by some people is to brand their opponents with names when they are unable to refute their arguments with facts and logic. Therefore, we find a few people of conservative thought who are inclined to brand every liberal view as Communistic. Likewise, we find some so-called liberals who stigmatize every conservative idea as fascistic. The utmost care, therefore, must be observed to distinguish clearly between what is obviously un-American and what is no more or less than an honest difference of opinion with respect to some economic, political, or social question.

But regardless of these protestations, Mr. Dies himself was responsible for much of the malpractice which today curses the nation. He had released a report by Edward E. Sullivan, committee investigator, but had to admit during a hearing, "He made the report, and we thought it advisable that the public should have the benefit of the report. We did not, at that time, and do not now vouch for its accuracy."

That was the beginning, apparently, of the release of unverified and unevaluated material which the public naturally assumed did represent information behind which the Committee stood.

Walter S. Steele of the *National Republic* who was chairman of the American Coalition Committee on National Safety testified, and placed the names of 640 organizations into the records as Communistic without a member questioning the validity of the accusations. Mr. Steele attacked the American Civil Liberties Union and the C.I.O. "All pacifists," says Father Ogden were relegated to the

common roll of dupes of communism, reaching such ridiculous
heights as the following section on Catholic associations, 'The radical
peace complex apparently has penetrated the Roman Catholic
Church.' "

Father Ogden writes,

At the beginning of the last year of its existence, the Dies Committee
received a new appropriation of $75,000. This, according to Cochran,
brought to $625,000 the amount granted the Committee since its inception.
At the time of this last grant, the Committee had on its payroll some
fourteen employees.

This scholarly Roman Catholic concludes,

Thinking men must admit that, if we use undemocratic means to
preserve our democracy, we, in the act of so doing, destroy that very
democracy. This study of the special House Committee for the Investigation of Un-American Activities indicates that the said Committee was
neither an ideal nor a desired means of exposing subversive activities.
It did not wholly fail in its endeavors, but, with different methods and
better procedure, it could have performed far more efficient service. Hence,
without disparaging the accomplishments of the Committee or impugning
the motives of any person connected with it, it must be admitted that
the history of the Committee reveals it to have failed in its essential purpose. It stands in the history of the House of Representatives as an example
of what an investigating committee should not be.

He recommends,

That a joint standing committee be created to maintain a continual
investigation of subversive affairs. It would have to be furnished enough
money to allow it to employ a staff of competent and disinterested investigators. . . . A method of collaboration with the F.B.I. should be provided
whereby not only the results of the investigations of the committee
would be made known to the Bureau, but conferences would be held in
advance to obviate the duplication of work by either body. It should be
understood that all matters relating to illegal activities should be left
to the Department of Justice, created for the enforcement of the laws of

the United States. Yet there would still remain many aspects of subversive activities that only a Congressional committee could thoroughly and competently expose. . . . Certain rules would have to be adopted. Among these would be a prohibition preventing any member of the committee, even its chairman, or any persons connected with it, from acting in its name or releasing any information unless the action had first been approved by a majority of the full committee. Steps would have to be taken to rule out hearsay and unreliable evidence by sifting the evidence and testing the credibility of witnesses in executive session. . . . In the hearings, no accusations would be permitted unless accompanied by proof. In all such cases, the accused individuals or organizations would be accorded an opportunity to appear before the committee within a reasonable limit of time. Cross-examination of all witnesses would be insisted upon, regardless of the type of evidence produced or the character of the witnesses. . . . It would have to have a system of procedure based upon respect for the individual rights of all citizens and consonant with the American tradition of fair play.[1]

I wished there were some way in which Father Ogden's study and that of Professor Carr entitled *The House Committee on Un-American Activities, 1945-1950,* could be placed in the hands of this Committee. My previous conversations with Mr. Kunzig had indicated that he had never read the volumes. I was quite certain that Congressmen like Bernard W. Kearney, Clyde Doyle, Morgan M. Moulder and James B. Frazier, Jr. would read such volumes carefully and be prepared to recommend proper reform. Other members of the Committee had not exhibited the teachable humility essential to learning. None the less, I was eager that Professor Carr's substantial study could be brought to their attention. Robert K. Carr is the Joel Parker Professor of Law and Political Science at Dartmouth College. His book was published by the Cornell University Press. It is one of the volumes in the Cornell Studies in Civil Liberty.

[1] Quotations from Father Ogden's book are used by permission of the Catholic University of America Press.

These research studies in civil liberties were made possible through a grant from the Rockefeller Foundation. In the concluding chapter entitled "The Committee's Record Evaluated," Professor Carr states:

On balance, the good things the Un-American Activities Committee has done are out-weighed by the bad. . . . All things considered, it appears that the record of the Un-American Activities Committee between 1945 and 1950 (and of the predecessor Dies Committee) is such that the wisest policy to follow would be the complete abolition of the Committee.

He is of the opinion that the threat of international communism might properly be the concern, as indeed it is, he says, of the Foreign Relations and Armed Services Committees of the two Houses. He thinks that these Committees can bring a greater measure of sophistication to an examination of the international Communist threat and are far better qualified to place the threat in its proper perspective than is the Un-American Activities Committee, and believes the Judiciary Committees of the two Houses would seem to be the proper watchdogs with respect to the threat of internal subversion.

On the substantive side, the greatest need is to delimit and define more carefully the subject matter under investigation. It is hard to say which is more unsatisfactory: the name of the Committee or the phraseology of the resolution setting forth its authority.

. . .

The substantive shortcomings in the Committee's record might be overcome by House action directing the Committee to concentrate upon a search for information concerning the adequacy of existing federal laws dealing with espionage, sedition, and sabotage, and concerning the enforcement of these laws by the executive agencies responsible for their administration.

He insists,

The House should force the Committee to cease altogether its efforts to demonstrate the "guilt" of particular individuals. The depersonalization of the work of the Un-American Activities Committee is the single most important change that is necessary if the threat offered by the Committee to the American way of life is to be overcome.

He holds,

Further delay in the formulation and adoption by Congress of sound, workable rules governing the organization and operation of its committees endangers the continuing usefulness and vitality of the investigating function—surely one of the most important functions of the Congress.

In stating the case for the Committee, Professor Carr points out, first, "the undeniable contribution it has made to the American people's understanding of the character and purposes of international Communism." But he adds that, "The Committee made this information available to the American people in such a disorderly and at times irresponsible way that the impact of its findings upon public opinion was much less than it might have been." Second, the Committee has helped to educate the American people concerning the purposes and methods of our own domestic Communist movement."

But again, more often than not, the Committee presented the information in such careless and irresponsible fashion that it failed to persuade honest men of the impartiality and importance of its findings. Third, the Committee has undoubtedly played a part in the exposure of espionage activities of Communist agents in the United States. It is seemingly true that neither Alger Hiss nor William Remington would ever have been prosecuted, had it not been for the investigations of the Committee, although it should also be noted that in each instance the prosecution was for perjury rather than espionage. Fourth, the Un-American Activities Committee may justly claim a major share of the credit for the passage by Congress of the Internal Security Act of 1950, in spite of the fact that the law takes its popular title from the name of the chairman of the Senate Judiciary Committee, Pat McCarran. [However,] it is one of the most criticized statutes in legislative history. Informed and impartial persons believe that it is an ill considered statute, many of whose provisions seriously endanger our fundamental freedoms.

The case against the Committee is set down as follows:

The most serious shortcoming in the Committee's record is the way it has always insisted on personalizing its undertakings. For centuries, we have believed that no man should be accused of an offense against society unless that offense has previously been carefully defined by law. We have further believed that an accused person shall be considered innocent until proved guilty, and that the state must assume the burden of the proof in demonstrating his guilt. Finally, we have believed that the state's attempt to demonstrate the accused's guilt must take place in a court of law, where the accused is allowed to enjoy such procedural rights as trial by jury, assistance of counsel, compulsory process for obtaining witnesses in his favor, and cross-examination of the witness against him.

Referring to the Committee between 1945 and 50, he says:

One of its leading purposes has been to demonstrate the "guilt" of certain persons for offenses not alway defined in law and to see them punished in the sense of the destruction of their reputations and the loss of their means of livelihood. It also had the much more simple role of driving such men from their jobs. For such a function to be exercised by such a poorly supervised and generally irresponsible body as the Un-American Activities Committee is a shocking thing.

The indictment continues:

The Committee has sometimes seemed more interested in exposing allegedly subversive persons than in exposing subversive activity. . . .

The House Committee must be held responsible for having encouraged a wide-spread witch-hunting spirit both in government and in private life. . . . It may further be asserted that McCarthyism would never have been possible, had not the Un-American Activities Committee and its predecessor, the Dies Committee, paved the way from 1938 on. . . . The House Committee has spawned a number of state committees which have eagerly joined in the hunt for disloyal Americans. . . .

The Committee has played a part in the demoralization of the federal service brought about by the emphasis of recent years upon loyalty testing. There is no doubt that in issuing his executive order in March, 1947, and establishing the federal loyalty program, President Truman acted to head off much more extreme demands being made by such Congressional agencies as the House Committee. . . . The activity of the House Committee has obstructed the recruitment of scientists into the public service. . . .

Another charge against the Committee is this:

By constantly exaggerating the subversive threat, the Committee has impaired the good judgment of many intelligent citizens. . . . The Committee has succeeded in discrediting the Congress of the United States in the eyes of many Americans. . . . The Committee has adversely affected the moral and intellectual atmosphere of the nation. . . . The Committee has made us distrustful of each other. . . . The Committee has also adversely affected the thinking of the nation by focusing attention almost exclusively upon the evil of Communism and almost totally ignoring the evils that produce Communism—such things as economic insecurity, racial discrimination, and social injustice.

When Mr. Dies was advocating the passage of the bill authorizing the House Committee on Un-American Activities, he said,

Let me say . . . that I believe all depends on the way the Committee is handled. I can conceive that a Committee constituted or composed of men whose object is to gain publicity, or whose object is to arouse some hatred against some race or creed, or to do things of that sort might do more harm than good. On the other hand, investigations have a useful purpose. . . . I am not in a position to say whether we can legislate effectively in reference to this matter, but I do know that exposure in a democracy of subversive activities is the most effective weapon that we have in our possession. Always we must keep in mind that in any legislative attempt to prevent un-American activities, we might jeopardize fundamental rights far more important than the objective we seek, but when these activities are exposed, when the light of day is brought to bear upon them, we can trust public sentiment in this country to do the rest.[2]

[2] Quotations from Professor Carr's book are used by permission of Cornell University Press.

As I sat waiting for the Committee to reconvene, I considered how the extreme "Americanism" of some Committeemen might be put into the record. Representative John Elliott Rankin once proposed a bill that would have rendered a teacher liable to a fine of ten thousand dollars and a prison term of ten years for "conveying the impression of sympathy with . . . communist ideology." Such distinguished men as William C. Bullitt, William Green, J. Edgar Hoover and Eric Johnston testified in opposition to such bills.

I wanted the Committee to know Professor Carr's evaluation of Mr. Steele's testimony:

It is possible that Steele's testimony was the most irresponsible ever presented to the Un-American Activities Committee. . . . [Steele's] unconscious revelation of the existence of a wide-spread vigilante movement in the United States is most disturbing. But the most shocking aspect of this hearing was the uncritical way in which the staff and members of the Un-American Activities Committee accepted everything that Steele said. Stripling went out of his way to indicate sweeping approval of the Steele data.

Mr. Stripling: Mr. Chairman, for the benefit of the record, we had Mr. Steele submit a list of those publications which we in turn submitted to our research department. The research department checked them with our files, and without a single exception all of them are either official organs of what the Committee considers to be Communist front organizations or an outright Communist publication.

Mr. Thomas said: Mr. Steele, in behalf of the Committee, the chair wants to express its appreciation of your coming here today and making the very complete statement that you have. In my eight years with this Committee, I have never seen a more complete, more documented statement on this subject than you have presented here today. You are to be congratulated for all of us. I just wanted to thank you very much.

Professor Carr is of the opinion that:

By and large, the Hollywood hearings revealed the Committee at its worst. In no other committee undertakings were the motivating forces of politics and the personal prejudices of the Committee members more apparent; in no other hearings were the over-all strategy and specific procedures more subject to criticism; no other major investigation committee ever ended so anti-climactically or produced so little tangible evidence in support of a thesis which the Committee set out to prove.

He was referring to the 1947 hearings, but adds,

In 1940, when the Committee was being run as a one man show by its increasingly reckless and irresponsible chairman, the motion picture industry was investigated in a series of closed hearings.

Jack L. Warner, referring to the filming of Ambassador Davies' book *Mission to Moscow,* said,

If making "Mission to Moscow" in 1942 was subversive activity, then the American Liberty ships which carried food and guns to Russia and the allies and the American Naval vessels which convoyed them were likewise engaged in subversive activities. The picture was made only to help a desperate war effort, and not for posterity.

When Louis B. Mayer, head of MGM, was on the stand, the Committee attacked him for producing *Song of Russia.* He said,

Mention has been made of the picture "Song of Russia" as being friendly to Russia at the time it was made. Of course it was. It was made to be friendly. . . . It was in April of 1942 that the story for "Song of Russia" came to our attention. It seemed a good medium of entertainment, and at the same time offered an opportunity for a pat on the back for our then ally, Russia. It also offered an opportunity to use the music of Tschaikovsky. We mentioned this to the government co-ordinators, and they agreed with us that it would be a good idea to make the picture. . . . The final script of "Song of Russia" was little more than a pleasant musical romance—the story of a boy and a girl that, except for the music of Tschaikovsky, might just as well have taken place in Switzerland, or England, or any other country on the earth.

Professor Carr's careful argument is balanced and impressive. He pays tribute where tribute is due. He says, "Under Nixon's leadership, the hearings were well conducted, with one exception. The atmosphere throughout was reasonably calm and judicial." This referred to the 1948 hearings.

He quotes the final report on Soviet Espionage in the United States, in which the Un-American Activities Committee asserts:

Communist espionage has broken through the security force of the United States government and made off with secret information of both military and diplomatic character concerning our national plans, policies, and actions and dates. . . . In this entirely accurate statement, the Committee points to its own achievement, for had it not been for the work of the Committee it is doubtful that any such statement of fact ever could have been made.

Referring to the conviction of Alger Hiss, Professor Carr points out,

In all, this record of achievement is a very considerable one. However . . . content as it seemingly was to stress only the sordid side of the story, it encouraged the irresponsible wave of Red-hunting and of loyalty-impugning which was to culminate early in 1950 in the shocking and dangerous tactics of Senator McCarthy.

What many people forget is the significant judgment Professor Carr records when he says,

None the less, it is a fact that the relentless search of recent years for subversive agents in the United States government has demonstrated beyond question the absolute loyalty of the overwhelming majority of the men and women who have labored in the Federal service during the war and post-war years.

An examination of the inadequate research on the part of the Committee staff in the case of Dr. Condon, the willingness of the Committee to listen with eagerness to the "ex-Communist turned informer," and its readiness to allow its material to be used by reactionary agencies for widespread attack upon liberals, are testimony to its inadequacy. The results of such practices were seen in their shameful menace in the Hazel Scott Powell hearing. Mrs. Powell protested because publications known as *Counter-Attack* and *Red Channels* had quoted statements from the California Committee on Un-American Activities she insisted were false. The Committee members argued that publication was not subject to criticism if it quoted such reports accurately. This meant that if the California Committee had made a false accusation the private agency publishing *Counter-Attack* was justified in republishing the falsehood, even though such publication might cost Mrs. Powell her job as an actress.

Mrs. Powell's rejoinder was devastating. She said, "May I ask you a question? If any committee, an official committee, lists me as having two heads, does that make me have two heads, and does that give *Red Channels* a right to publish I have two heads?" *Red Channels* was a publication listing people in the entertainment and radio field who were alleged to be subversive.

The Committee objected to her indignant criticism of a private agency that had published what she declared to be a lie.

But there were other vitally important questions that should have been considered.

The Great Seal of the United States should never be used to validate incompetency. Disrespect for the flag is properly punished. The use of the Great Seal upon some of the publications of the House Committee on Un-American Activities is unforgivable. A code governs the display of the flag. The Seal ought to be similarly protected. I do not object to Congressional investigation. As a matter of fact, upon scores of occasions, I have stated there is a proper and necessary place for the Congressional investigating committee. Again and again, I have stated that much good has come from some investigations. My request for a hearing was in no sense an attempt to challenge the right of investigation. It was to bring to light the rejection of American procedures and the damage to American citizens resulting from the irresponsible issuance of unverified items arranged in such fashion as to incriminate. It was to protest against the indifference of men who, acting outside the law, refused to revise releases so as to tell the truth. It was to protest against practices by some Congressmen who chameleonlike have taken on totalitarian coloration. Conform or die is the dictate of the demagogue. Think and let think is the proclamation of the democrat. Committeemen, who set themselves in judgment upon other Americans, who are party to the undermining of reputation and the creation of a society in which men whisper instead of speak, have departed from the traditions of America and are stifling American creativity and suffocating the freedom upon which it depends. The American has been proud of diversity. He has refused to be shackled by dogmatism. He has been a free man in a free society ready to discover and act upon the truth that frees. Gauleiters and commissars are the rank growth of the fascist and communist society. They are obnoxious weeds to be torn up by the roots and cast into the fire. Contemporary threats to civil liberty must be faced. Our history includes the record of numerous struggles to abridge the liberties of the American people, and of the refusal of the Americans to bow to tyranny. A free spirit has always triumphed, whether in the conflict with the Alien and Sedition Acts of long ago or the illegal practices of the Department of Justice under Attorney General Palmer of yesterday.

I have said I believe the Communist Party is a conspiracy. I believe conspirators should be discovered, tried under due process, and if found guilty, punished. The issue that is before us, and was before us in this hearing, was not the propriety of Congressional investigations nor was it a question concerning the existence of a Communist conspiracy. It was solely a question of procedures of a Committee in which the rights of individuals and disregard for civil liberties are undermined. I had hoped there might be some opportunity to document the incompetency and inefficiency of the Committee research staff upon which the Committee members relied, and that out of such documentation might come sound reform. I had hoped to point out the inefficiency that has characterized the so-called organization of this Committee.

There has been a high turnover in Committee personnel. Between 1945 and 1950, twenty-two different Representatives served upon this Committee. It had three chairmen and at least two acting chairmen, and its staff had four chiefs. Has any other committee of the Congress witnessed such frequent change in personnel? Some able men have served upon this Committee, but, in the large, it has not been noted for the high quality of its membership.

Congressman Rankin, who held deep prejudices against the Jews and the Negroes, was for a considerable time a powerful factor in this Committee. Speaking on the floor of the House of Representatives on July 18, 1945, he said, "Communism . . . hounded and persecuted a Saviour during his earthly ministry, inspired his crucifixion, derided him in his dying agony, and then gambled for his garments at the foot of the Cross. . . . These alien-minded Communistic enemies of Christianity and their stooges, are trying to get control of the press of the country. Many of our great daily newspapers have now changed hands and gone over to them. . . . They are trying to take over the radio. Listen to their lying broadcasts in broken English and you can almost smell them." No wonder the Committee has, at times, been party to the spread of false witness. It is refreshing to record Professor Carr's estimate of Vice President Nixon. He wrote, "It is not hard to over-praise Nixon, for he brought to the Committee enthusiasm, willingness to work hard, ability as a lawyer, and a reasonable detachment and sense of fairness, qualities that had been rare among the Committee's members."

As I sat there through the day, I realized that this Committee, if it would give but ten days' careful study to the files, could rectify the abuses, but public speeches made by some of them and numerous letters written by several of them indicated an unwillingness to face the facts and a determination to silence critics.

The incompetency of the Committee procedures could be proved. It was clearly revealed in the attack Congressman Velde made upon Mrs. Agnes E. Meyer. It was this attack that prompted me to speak out upon this issue at the inauguration of Dr. Hurst R. Anderson as president of the American University, an address that occasioned Congressman Jackson's disgraceful performance upon the floor of the House of Representatives. Mrs. Meyer, a courageous, patriotic, competent citizen had delivered an address before the American Association of School Superintendents. In it, she had dealt with the threat to education that lies in the unwarranted attacks and procedures of some investigating committees. She was specific and mentioned Senators McCarthy and Jenner and Congressman Velde. What did Mr. Velde do? Instead of attempting to answer her arguments in dignified fashion and relying upon truth to convince the public, he announced that Mrs. Meyer had contributed an article to *Soviet Russia Today*. He had succumbed to the disease that afflicts the research staff. It is contagious, and he apparently possessed no immunity. He sought to answer Mrs. Meyer by linking her name with a magazine alleged to be under Communist influence. But he had not reckoned with Mrs. Meyer. She is not only a woman of extraordinary ability, but a woman of wealth and very great influence. She checked the matter and was able to prove she had never written such an article. It had been written by a woman named Mayer. The difference in spelling had escaped the "research" staff. Mrs. Mayer did not live in Washington, D.C. She lived, I believe, in British Columbia which may have been confused with the state of Washington by the investigator whose training might not have included geography. Mr. Velde had to apologize. He announced that he had dismissed the investigator who was responsible for the erroneous information. I could have felt relieved had he long ago dismissed those who had given the Committee misinformation concerning me. The point, however, is that a chairman of the Committee was let down in public by information given to him by a staff so incompetent that it did not properly check before reporting to its chief.

A second instance was to be found in my own file. John S. Wood, the former chairman of the Committee, sent me a copy of the file that had been released by the Committee in which it was alleged I had written an article on Stalin. The paper, the date and the page were cited. I had not written it. I secured the paper, had it photostated and sent to Mr. Wood. He apologized and assured me that while this was an error there was no intent to harm me. But the harm had been done. I have received many letters from many states condemning me for having written an article I had never written. The condemnation was based upon the release of files incompetently prepared or deliberately slanted.

A third illustration would have sufficed to prove the incompetency with which I charged them. In 1948, the Committee published a pamphlet entitled *Communism and Religion.* On page 15, question 92 is asked, "What is the Methodist Federation for Social Action?" Answer, "A tool of the Communist Party, denounced by numerous loyal American Methodists." On May 10, 1951, John S. Wood, then chairman of the House Committee, wrote a letter in which he stated, "This Committee has made no investigation of The Methodist Federation for Social Service, or its successor, The Methodist Federation for Social Action, and therefore is unable to furnish you information in regard to that organization." A report is published in 1948 announcing a conclusion. In 1951, we learn that no investigation of the organization has been made. This is incompetency. I knew that the Committee had published a report entitled "Review of The Methodist Federation for Social Action, formerly The Methodist Federation for Social Service." I knew that no member of the Federation had been interviewed. No careful study had been made of its history.

A thoroughgoing study which had been submitted for the doctor's degree in philosophy to Boston University was available. Apparently, the investigators had never heard of it. I knew that an official commission of the Methodist Church had given eight years of study to this question and had reported to the General Conference of the Methodist Church in 1932. Its chairman was the late Bishop Adna Wright Leonard who was killed in an air crash during the war when on service to his government. He was a conservative leader of great influence. This report is not mentioned in the so-called "Review."

The House Committee report begins with the statement that there had been a demand for this study. The demand is not identified. The report is described as "a careful and studied review of the information . . . that is available to the Committee." It begins with the astounding statement that "while the Methodist Federation for Social Service was founded in 1907, information in the files of this Committee begins with the year of 1928." On page three, instead of stating the full objective of the Federation, it quotes but half of the objective and gives a false understanding of its true purpose. I myself had resigned from the Federation for reasons that I believed to be sound, but I cannot tolerate stupid misrepresentations that appear in this review and which are testimony to the inadequate work done by the investigators of this Committee. This "Review" is composed of newspaper clippings, lengthy quotations from a small county newspaper published in Princeton, Illinois, a series of articles by Frederick Woltman of *The World-Telegram*, and articles from *The Chicago Tribune*. Page after page is given to a criticism of the organization, that appeared in 1932, by George B. Lockwood of the *National Republic*. Stanley High's article is featured. After sixty-five pages of such "research," the Committee includes three pages written by Dean Walter G. Muelder of the Boston University School of Theology, the vice president of the organization, entitled "What About the Methodist Federation?" Instead of coming to a conclusion, which might have been helpful to readers, the "Review" ends with the statement, "Information in the files of this Committee is not too clear as to when the Methodist Federation for Social Service became the Methodist Federation for Social Action." A letter written to the Federation would have brought that "vital" information. But the "Review" is climaxed with this enlightening paragraph, "The record of these two organizations as presented herein may be of some aid to those who are interested in determining whether the Federation has been favorable to, or supported Communist objectives."

It was not until 1953 that the Committee appears to have gone into the publications of the Federation with any care. At that time, Mr. Benjamin Gitlow, a former Communist, testified before the Committee and sought to present an analysis of its publications. Was he paid for his services? If so, by whom? Referring to a request that appeared in the Bulletin of the Federation calling upon its members to protest against a "holy war against the Soviet Union," Mr. Gitlow stated, "Neither Bishop Lewis O. Hartman, the Federation's President, and Bishops G. Bromley Oxnam and James C. Baker, the Federation's Vice Presidents, objected." How did Mr. Gitlow know this? As a matter of fact, he knew nothing of the kind. I hold no brief for the Methodist Federation for Social Action. I testified during the hearing that I believed it had been unwisely and improperly led by the Reverend Jack McMichael and that I had resigned from it. It is to point out that a massing of unevaluated material and its publication in a review, without so much as conferring with the parties involved nor the agency under discussion, is inexcusable.

◀ VII ▶

I protest against the apparent determination of the Committee to save face rather than to face facts. I protest against its unwillingness to clean up its files and to revise its procedures so as to eliminate its abuses. Neither ignorance nor inertia can longer be tolerated. Congressmen, who have introduced bills designed to bring investigating committee procedures into harmony with American tradition, deserve the support of the public whose patience is well-nigh exhausted.

WITH the Committee reassembled, my reveries came to a sudden end. I resented the fact that the Committee wasted public money and the time of a private citizen. I knew Morris L. Ernst and David Loth in *Report on the American Communist* in a concluding chapter of but twenty pages present more constructive suggestions designed to defeat the Communist Party in the United States than are contained, I believe, in all the publications of the House Committee on Un-American Activities. They recommend that a national program for combating communism should include proposals for speeding "the sincere voluntary withdrawal of members and for disillusioning the susceptible before they enter the Party rather than afterwards." This proposal seeks to deprive the Communist Party of members and is based upon a reasonable assumption that almost all of the rank and file members under thirty years of age could be drawn away from communism. They believe that a national program should be based upon certain fundamental principles.

1. That the nation's steady progress toward economic and social justice should not be checked by hysterical outcries that Communists support or pretend to support measures which speed that progress.

2. That we reject the Communist self-appraisal of their own movement as based on economic truths; at the same time we recognize that membership in this country is not comparable to that in some other countries where it is based on hunger and despair, and therefore promise of mere subsistence or an acre of land has no appeal. In our land the movement is not a belly movement.

3. That since American Communists are motivated largely by psychological factors, these same factors must be used decisively in combating them.

4. That the bulwarks of American freedom, which are far more important than any other ideology to the welfare of the people, should not be sacrificed through the frantic expedient of burning the house down to get rid of the rats, if for no better reason than that we know rats live in ruins even more happily than in the house.

The present trend drives the Party underground. Thus, instead of laws that involve more secrecy, they recommend laws that lead to light. They say, "Except for overt acts of the nature of treason and sabotage—for which we have ample protection in law—the real danger of any organization seeking to overthrow American institutions stems from stealth." And they insist that "no subversive movement has made much headway through open advocacy."

They believe we can meet the Communist in the open market of ideas and support a recommendation of the President's Committee on Civil Rights, under the chairmanship of Charles E. Wilson, namely,

The principle of disclosure is, we believe, the appropriate way to deal with those who would subvert our democracy by revolution or by encouraging disunity and destroying the civil rights of some groups. We have considered and rejected proposals which have been made to us for censoring or prohibiting material which defames religious or racial minority groups. Our purpose is not to constrict anyone's freedom to speak; it is rather to enable the people better to judge the true motives of those who try to sway them.

They, therefore, insist upon legislation which will require groups that seek to influence public opinion to tell who they are, what they work for, and who supports them. This principle underlies the procedures of the Securities and Exchange Commission, the Federal Trade Commission, and the Pure Food and Drug Administration. This principle of disclosure must apply to all groups and not be restricted to certain categories of ideas.

Messrs. Ernst and Loth recommend the creation of a nonpartisan commission to spend a year in studying how to prevent subversion without destroying freedom. They believe that police work is necessary if we are going to be protected from Communist conspiracy and that such police work should be left entirely in the hands of the government agency best equipped to carry it out, namely, the F.B.I.

They recommend a program which will open up employment for former Communists who sincerely repudiate the movement and wish to be separated from it forever, and in this endeavor believe that labor unions, service clubs and organizations of employers could be most effective. The Veterans Associations are in the position to be most helpful by backing a nation-wide program of education, but we are warned that "when they set themselves up as judges of opinion, finding people guilty by association or even branding them as Reds because of liberal views, they are not only committing gross injustice but are playing into the hands of the Communist Party."

Schools and colleges have a vital role to play in exposing the nature of communism, and through the schools the students should learn the truth about communism. They urge that the individual should keep informed about the organizations to which he belongs, that he should disavow all vigilante groups, no matter how powerful in the community. He should demand "overwhelming evidence, after proper hearings, before branding an organization or an industry, or an individual as Communist." They reject smears of non-Communists and should recognize and welcome the change of heart that does occur.

Their fundamental recommendation is persistent campaign on behalf of our positive beliefs. The approach is too largely negative. We must, and can, take the initiative.

Mr. Kunzig turned again to his list of exhibits.

The introduction of exhibits is like a sleight-of-hand act in which the magician proves that the hand is faster than the eye.

"Exhibit No. 10," followed by "Exhibit No. 11," and so on, created the illusion of weighty evidence. Actually, the material was at times improperly identified, and was generally irrelevant and immaterial.

If I were to testify again, I would demand time to examine every exhibit and take time to indicate its specious or spurious character. I noted the impression that the introduction of supposed exhibits was making, but, denied the privilege of objecting, I did not at the time know how to cope with this ruse.

Mr. Kunzig had originally introduced Exhibit 1, which was an article that had appeared in the Washington *Post,* entitled "A Velde File Dissected." It was a condensation of a carefully prepared analysis of the file this Committee had released from time to time. I should have insisted that it be read, so that the Committee, together with the audience in the hearing room and the nation-wide television and radio audience might have heard the answers to the falsehoods that the file had contained. Fortunately, these answers are in the record. The file that was so dissected was the file released during recent years. It differs from the earlier releases that had gone so far as to contain expressions of opinion by the clerk and admonitions to the recipient. The file Mr. Kunzig introduced left out the section that alleged I had written an article upon Stalin.

Some experienced journalists were confused by the clever device of introducing exhibits. It was below the belt fighting, but there is no referee in such bouts.

A "morning after" analysis of the exhibits reveals that there are 48 in the record. Of the 48, I introduced 12. Thus, the counsel had introduced 36 exhibits. Ten of them were nothing more than newspaper clippings, five of which came from the Los Angeles *Times* of 1923; one was an advertisement from the Los Angeles *News*, announcing that I was to address the Forum of the First Unitarian Church. Of the four remaining, two were from *The Daily Worker*, one from *The New York Times*, and one from the *San Francisco Chronicle*. Three of the four included my name as sponsoring a meeting I had never sponsored and had never attended. The other listed me as having signed a petition I had never signed. How many hours and how much public money had been spent collecting these clippings, I do not know.

Thirteen of the 36 exhibits were letterheads. Several of the letterheads were of the same organization. Actually, these letterheads referred to eight agencies. Five of the eight were never cited as subversive by the Attorney General. In the five was the letterhead of the Board of Missions and Church Extension of the Methodist Church. One was the letterhead of an agency with which I had nothing whatsoever to do. Thus, we were back to the two, namely, the Council of American-Soviet Friendship and Medical Aid for Spain.

Of the remaining exhibits, one was a dodger which had advertised me to speak at a meeting I had refused to attend, and of course did not address. Another was a bibliography, introduced because a book that the Board of Missions and Church Extension had recommended, written by Vera Micheles Dean, had been included. Because this bibliography had been issued by the National Council on American-Soviet Friendship, the book itself was therefore alleged to be tainted.

There were three press releases. I had had no relationship whatsoever to two of them, and have no recollection of having approved the third.

There was a booklet written by the greatly loved and highly honored Dr. Louie B. Newton, pastor of the Druid Hills Baptist Church of Atlanta, Georgia, former president of the Southern Baptist Convention. He had written the story of his visit to Russia, accompanied by the Reverend Dr. Ralph W. Sockman, and others, and I had written an introduction to the pamphlet. Then, there were four magazine exhibits. One was an article written by Miss Winifred Chappell in 1934, for which I had no responsibility and with which I totally disagreed. Two referred to *The Protestant* magazine, and one to an article I had contributed to *Soviet Russia Today*.

What does it all add up to?

But to come back to Mr. Kunzig and Mr. Jackson and their exhibits.

The fact that the Committee had released files, but would assume no responsibility for their accuracy, and had failed to inform readers of this fact, stood out like a sore thumb. Mr. Jackson tried to explain this. He said, somewhat lamely:

> I believe that—and I am willing to report on this—the absence of the general disclaimer . . . was due to the fact you had the opportunity to go over the material.

He added:

> I might say that disclaimer is now a part of the first page of every report that is going out, which meets the objection, or one of the objections, which you have proposed. . . . There was an element of censorship on the report—and I don't know when that has happened in any other case, with the exception of yours.

The truth is, there had been no such censorship. The files had been released from 1946. It was not until 1951 that any of my denials had been so much as referred to in a file. It was necessary to respond to Mr. Jackson's statement. I tried to be courteous, and expressed appreciation, but had to say, "Unfortunately, it is not in accord with the fact."

Mr. Jackson had stated that the inclusion of the disclaimer is "currently a policy of the Committee." I pointed out that the Chairman of the Committee himself, as late as March 31, 1953, had sent out the full file without any disclaimer attached to it.

Mr. Walter, unpredictable and at times irrelevant, broke in with, "Are you under the mistaken impression that the law imposes upon us the duty to look only into Communist activities?"

I replied that I thought the term was more inclusive, that it was "Un-American Activities."

There was an insulting implication in his reply. "We are concerned with activities that aid and abet Communist movements and with people who assist Communist movements, wittingly or unwittingly. I am not going to express my own opinion about your membership in these organizations, but we are concerned with the machinations of the Communist Party which result in naïve people fronting all sorts of activities which have as their ultimate result the destruction of our republican form of government."

It is apparent that these men had come to the hearing convinced that the unfounded accusations of their research staff were true. I had tried to make it clear throughout the day that I had not belonged to such organizations. It was hard to take Mr. Walter's insinuations.

I said, "Well, you see, both of my sons were overseas."

He interrupted, "Well, I am not interested in that."

I continued, "—in the Army."

He said, "I don't care whether they were or not."

I continued, "—and I want—"

Once again, in bad manners, he broke in, "So let's not get off on a tangent every time a question is asked."

I replied, "I am not getting off on a tangent. I am going to ask, if I may, sir, why a report on the National Council of the Churches of

Christ in the U.S.A. is released by this body without the kind of disclaimer that is said to accompany all of the reports now."

Mr. Velde interjected that all of this information was public and all of it could be secured from the Congressional Library anyhow.

I said, "Mr. Chairman, I have never objected to that. I have objected to the release of it before it is verified. Surely, this great Committee when it puts something out on its letterhead involving an individual would wish to verify it before it puts it out, even though it says that it is public information. When you list that I wrote an article on Stalin which I did not write, the Congressional Library does not have information to that effect."

Mr. Moulder said, "As I understand the Bishop, it is your contention that the issuance of that information amounts to a verification because of its release by the Committee on Un-American Activities. Is that your contention, that it amounts to an indirect verification?"

I replied, "Quite. When it is put out on the letterhead of this Committee with Congress back of it, people understandably believe that it represents an opinion, unless the disclaimer is clearly there, and it hasn't been there in my case and in many others."

I then asked Mr. Velde, "Mr. Chairman, for my own information, and I'm very sincere here—what is the purpose of releasing this public information, for which the Committee does not vouch? What is its purpose?"

Mr. Velde said, "This information is not released by the Committee. It has been released previously."

I replied, "Well, it is released when it goes out in connection with your letterhead."

Mr. Velde thought he was on firm ground when he said, "In response to a question a while ago, you indicated that you didn't know about your being listed on letterheads of certain organizations until you learned through our files that you were listed. I feel you, as a good American citizen, should appreciate the fact that our Committee made this knowledge about you available."

I replied, "I do appreciate it, but would have appreciated it more if you had sent it to me instead of releasing it to others, because it has been used by private agencies. I will not mention them here, but one private agency has used this material seriously to harm one's reputation—and it got it from this Committee. That's what I'm getting at, sir."

Mr. Walter wanted to know what these agencies were. I named the American Council of Christian Churches, for one, and the so-called American Council of Christian Laymen headed by Vern Kaub. He wanted to know what other private agencies. I told him I could list twenty. I said, "The American Council of Churches is an organization, I should judge, of about 170,000 people, perhaps."

"What object would they have in using files of the Committee on Un-American Activities to injure you?"

I said, "I'll be glad to answer that, if the chairman will allow me to do so." I started to explain what the American Council of Churches really was, and compared it to the National Council of Churches, but apparently they did not want to get into this field. They called it an "inter-faith discussion."

Mr. Walter could not understand why I called the churches "private agencies." I said, "To make it clear that they are not governmental agencies." That seemed to satisfy him.

Then Mr. Kunzig, with the full knowledge that his Committee is of record concerning the American Civil Liberties Union, brought up that question again.

On October 23, 1939, the official record of the Committee on Un-American Activities reads:

This Committee found last year in its report that there was not any evidence that the American Civil Liberties Union was a Communist organization. That being true, I do not see why we would be justified in going into it again—into it, I mean, after all, they have been dismissed by unanimous report of the Committee as a Communist organization.

These words were spoken by Mr. Dies during a session of the Committee.

On February 17, 1952, the Committee in an official report said:

The American Civil Liberties Union has never been cited as being red-dominated or as Communist by any official organization charged with the duty of investigating subversive activities.

Did Mr. Kunzig think that he could cast suspicion upon me by such a query?

I said, "I believe it to be one of the organizations of this country rendering very valuable service in the maintenance of the civil liberties of this country, and if there were time, I would like to read into the record statements from Thomas E. Dewey concerning it, from General MacArthur concerning it, from President Truman, from General Lucius D. Clay, and men of that kind, including a message sent by the President of the United States, President Eisenhower, to a recent meeting where several of the agencies standing for civil liberties, I believe, were meeting in Philadelphia, a message from the President commending these agencies for what they are doing. I am a member of it."

Mr. Kunzig's purpose was to show that Professor Harry F. Ward had been the head of the American Civil Liberties Union.

MR. KUNZIG: "You know he [Professor Ward] is a good friend of yours; is that right?"

I replied, "Just a minute. Don't put answers in my mouth, please."

MR. KUNZIG: "Just answer the question."

I said, "I will."

He then asked, "Is he a good friend of yours?"

I said, "I will have to answer that question by telling you when he was and what my relationship is with him now. Professor Ward came to the Boston University School of Theology, I believe, in 1914. I was a student. He was a brilliant teacher. He was an inspirational personality. He made an extraordinary contribution to the students of that institution. I was very, very fond of him. I took dictation from him as a part-time secretary in the dictation of one of his books. I knew his family. Professor Ward was a leader in the social movement of the Methodist Church, and over a long period of time rendered, I believe, very valuable service.

"There came a time in my mind when I believed that Professor Ward had shifted his views concerning the whole Communist question. I found myself in fundamental disagreement with Professor Ward as early as 1928.

"In 1932, I had to propose, I believe—no, it was 1928 that I proposed the message that was drafted by the Methodist Church for the Resolution on the social question. It was in opposition to Professor Ward's proposal; but what I proposed was carried by the Methodist Church.

"In 1936, I drafted the resolution that put the Methodist Church on record as one of the earliest denominations in opposition to Communism and to Fascism. We were, but nobody had ever said that before, and I wanted it in a clear resolution.

"From 1936—and I'm not sure I saw Professor Ward even then— I've seen Professor Ward once, I know, since 1936—I think probably since 1932.

"Now, then, he was an inspirational teacher, to whom I owe very, very much. He was a dear personal friend. When he shifted his views, as I believed, I had to break with Professor Ward. He understood it.

"I can bring for the Committee, if it wishes, the letters that I wrote to him back at that time indicating a complete break in the matter of what he was standing for and what I believed we should stand for.

"So, when you ask me if he is my friend, I can't say yes or no to that. I have to recount this, and Professor Ward was a member of the American Civil Liberties Union, and when that organization—"

Mr. Kunzig interrupted, "He was the head of it at that time, wasn't he?"

I replied, "Yes. Well, I don't know whether he was in '23. He may have been. I don't know, but what I am saying is that in 1940 when the American Civil Liberties Union took action barring anyone who believes in totalitarianism from the organization, Professor Ward resigned in protest, which indicated, I think, his attitude upon several matters; and I believe others were expelled from the organization. It was one of the first organizations, I think, to take action barring Communists really from its membership."

Mr. Kunzig said, "Now this same Professor Ward was also head of the Union Theological Seminary, is that right?"

I replied, "No, sir. He was a professor in the Union Theological Seminary."

MR. KUNZIG: "And a most influential one?"

I said, "He was a professor there. I wouldn't say 'most.' There are many men there. It has a distinguished faculty. When you have men like Reinhold Niebuhr and men of that kind, you don't use the word 'most' in regard to any of the faculty."

Then Mr. Clardy said, "I have mentioned repeatedly, witness, the testimony which is about to be released. I want to direct your attention to one portion of it, that portion which specifically says that when the Communist Party was organized in 1919, Dr. Ward was already a convinced Communist, with a few insignificant, minor reservations. I am quoting verbatim from the testimony by Benjamin Gitlow, who was one of the founders and organizers of the Communist Party in the United States. Now, I shall not go on beyond that, except to direct your attention to that part, because immediately following the portion I have read to you—and it will be possibly in the first 15 pages or so of that part of the transcript devoted to his testimony because it is on page 29 of the typewritten—is a delineation of the part that Dr. Ward—Rev. Dr. Ward—followed in connection with the Syndicalist and other movements. I ask you to read that particularly, because you will discover through all that time of your association with him he was a Communist."

Mr. Clardy had pronounced judgment upon the basis of an accusation made by a former Communist. Professor Ward had not been heard. Professor Ward subsequently denied ever having been a member of the Communist Party. But on the testimony of professional witnesses, this man, trained in the law, reaches and announces a conclusion based upon a single accusation.

The purpose was clear. Extensive hearings in New York had preceded my hearing. There is reason to believe the purpose was to uncover material which it was hoped would implicate me. The hearing of course failed of this objective.

I wondered at the time how long this Committee could fool the people. President Lincoln was right. I knew some of the people could be fooled some of the time; but I could not believe all of them could be fooled all of the time.

Here was an attempt to show that I had been associated with the Methodist Federation for Social Action, that Professor Ward was in it, and that he, according to these professional witnesses, had been a Communist all along. People would draw the inference that I must have known that he was a Communist, and therefore sympathized with the Communist view.

Did these men want the truth? Did they understand the meaning of investigation? My books and articles were of record: my activities were reasonably well known. I would have been happy to have conferred with their representatives or with them. It appeared to me they were determined to strike down a critic.

An investigating committee that had published a bulletin upon the Methodist Federation for Social Action should have studied its organization, and should have known that it was loosely set up, as are many church organizations, that it had been organized in 1907, ten years before the Russian Revolution and twenty-five years before the New Deal, that an official Commission of the church reporting on its work in 1932 had stated, "Our study of the work of the Methodist Federation for Social Service leads us to the conclusion that the peculiar and exceedingly important work which has been undertaken by this body of Methodists can best be prosecuted through an agency organized and operated in the manner which has characterized this Federation during the last quarter of a century."

The report stressed the fact that "the Federation does not speak, nor does it attempt to speak, officially for the church" and concluded, "The commendations of this social agency which have, from time to time, been given by the General Conference, have been fully justified."

The relation of the five thousand members to the agency was largely that of individuals who received the Bulletin that came out once a month. Once a year, there would be an annual meeting at which the members present discussed every kind of question, debated them, and came to their own conclusions.

I pointed out that during the time I was vice president, I attended but two or three meetings.

In the present circumstances, it is clear that one ought to belong to fewer organizations and know them intimately and participate fully in the formulation of their policy. The Federation for a quarter of a century had enjoyed the participation of outstanding leaders of the church, and while raising questions upon which there was fundamental difference of opinion, none the less had rendered valuable service. This was in large measure true until the Reverend Jack McMichael became executive secretary. The Federation had been, as I testified, "a body that was raising questions constantly, out in front of the church. The church went as fast as it wished to go, but we felt this group out there raising social questions was rendering service."

Mr. Kunzig introduced page after page of testimony concerning Professor Ward, the Methodist Federation for Social Action, and the Reverend Jack McMichael. He wanted to know what my relation to the Federation had been. That was a proper question. I told him I had been a member of the Federation from student days, and when I went to New York City to become Bishop there, I had been elected a vice president, and that I had resigned on June 9, 1947, as vice president and as a member of the Executive Committee.

He then wanted to know if I had ever been executive secretary of the organization. This brings up again the incompetency of research. He had a letterhead. If he had taken five minutes to dictate a letter to me and had asked for information, he could have received it long before. I was never executive secretary of the organization. When the Methodist Federation for Social Service celebrated its twentieth anniversary, a special committee was appointed to plan for that celebration. Dr. Ernest F. Tittle, one of the truly great preachers in the history of the Methodist Church, was appointed chairman. I was appointed secretary. When the letterhead came out, I noted that my name was listed as "Executive Secretary" of the committee that was to plan for the anniversary. I had never had an executive relationship with the Federation, and a careful reading of the letterhead itself would have made that clear.

I explained the vice presidency by saying, "That was largely a nominal matter, I was not present at the meeting, and the name continued until there was good reason for me to resign from the Federation, which I did."

Mr. Kunzig then tried to play his trump card. He asked, "Now, the Executive Secretary at that time, on the same letterhead with you, is Jack Richard McMichael. Do you know Jack McMichael?—do you know him to be a member of the Communist Party?"

I replied, "I did not know that he was a member of the Communist Party, but I found myself in such fundamental opposition to Jack McMichael that I had to face one of two decisions, either to stay in and get him out or to get out myself, and it seemed to me wiser to resign and sever all relations because I was a little fearful it would take a bit longer to get him out than I had time to give."

Mr. Clardy, quoting from the testimony of Benjamin Gitlow, stressed the fact that McMichael had been identified as a member of the Party. The Reverend Jack McMichael was later to appear before the Committee and to deny this under oath. I myself pointed out that the Reverend Jack McMichael was being condemned in public before he had been heard; and questioned the propriety of such procedure.

Referring to the Gitlow testimony, I said, "Mr. Chairman, since this has been read, may I say that I did everything that I could to get McMichael out of the organization. Certain information reached me to this effect. I talked to Mr. McMichael. He said that it was absolutely false, and wanted the source of the information. I was unable to give him that source, because it was confidential. We had—"

Mr. Velde said, "Bishop, may I interrupt? Why did you attempt to get him out of the organization?"

I answered, "Because, frankly, I believed that Jack McMichael was so tied up with the Communist group that whether or no he were a Communist, I couldn't prove whether he was a member of the Communist Party or not, but I was sure that that organization ought not to be under that leadership any more, and I did everything I could. Others talked to Mr. McMichael. He denied this completely. Now, that raises quite an issue, sir."

REPRESENTATIVE WALTER: "Will you yield at that point?"

BISHOP OXNAM: "Yes."

REPRESENTATIVE WALTER: "What caused you to reach the conclusion that McMichael was a Communist?"

BISHOP OXNAM: "Sir, I hope you will not press that question. I will be glad to state it to this Committee if I could meet it in executive session. The source of that information was strictly confidential, and I think I would be betraying a trust if I said it in public. I would be glad to convey it to the chairman of this Committee. I am not hedging here at all, but I think I have an obligation because the source was of such a nature—I think the chairman would be the first to recognize this. I will not refer to the source other than that."

REPRESENTATIVE WALTER: "You couldn't make it much plainer."

REPRESENTATIVE VELDE: "I don't think the witness should be required to answer except in executive session. We appreciate that."

BISHOP OXNAM: "I will be very happy, sir, to give you the source of that."

REPRESENTATIVE SCHERER: "Bishop, at the time you got this information that Reverend McMichael was a member of the Communist Party, you reported it to the F.B.I., did you?"

BISHOP OXNAM: "It was not necessary to report it there. Don't misunderstand me, sir. I am trying to keep a confidence here which I will be glad—"

REPRESENTATIVE WALTER: "You have said it very well, I assure you."

I then pointed out that "in the Methodist Church when any individual has information that justifies prosecution and the elimination of an individual from the Church, he may report it to what we call an investigating committee, and if there is ground for charges, the charges are formulated, and he is tried.

"Now, there are members of this Committee who are members of the Methodist Church and have that information. It would have been possible with that information, which we do not have, to have filed charges and to have prosecuted Jack McMichael. He would have been removed from the Methodist ministry if there could have been evidence of the fact of belonging to the Communist Party. By that I mean a man must be disloyal to his ordination vows to be a Communist, which involves being an atheist."

REPRESENTATIVE SCHERER: "He is still a Methodist minister today, is he not?"

BISHOP OXNAM: "Yes, sir, and if somebody will give us the evidence that he belongs to the Communist Party, charges will be filed against him—this is the first time we have ever heard anything, and please remember, this is simply testimony. We have not heard the answers yet. I take it for granted this is true from what I have heard, but it is not the way we do things in a Methodist court. It would have to be proved."

REPRESENTATIVE VELDE: "Bishop, the Committee, of course, cannot vouch for the veracity of any of the witnesses that come before it. This is merely—"

BISHOP OXNAM: "I am sure that is true, but the assumption is that what is said is true, you see, and in one of our courts you would have to have not only the statement, but you would have to have the proof."

REPRESENTATIVE JACKSON: "This is testimony under oath, of course, testimony taken under oath."

BISHOP OXNAM: "Of course."

Mr. Kunzig now turned his questioning to Professor Ward and his ideas.

Mr. Walter asked, "During what period of time did you have the suspicion that he was a Communist while he was acting as a theological professor in Boston University and at Union?"

I replied, "I did not believe he was a Communist. I did not believe he was a Communist when he was at the Boston University School of Theology. I do not know he is a Communist now. This testimony is quite overwhelming, but when Dr. Ward went to Russia and came back and wrote a book called *In Place of Profit* I began to have serious intellectual doubts because in that, if I recall correctly, he justified a lottery on the grounds that it was contributing to a certain valuable social end. Well, when a man's ethics begin to be as confused as that, something has happened somewhere, and that is the best answer I can give, sir."

I thought it wise to turn these questions from the views of someone not before the Committee to the views of the one who was sitting as witness. So I said, "Mr. Chairman, I know we must get on, but when I returned from Russia in 1934, I put down ten impressions of the situation as I found it. I do not know whether the Committee would appreciate for the record those critical impressions of one who went there trying to study or not, but they do explain my personal attitude. I would not wish to read them, but I think they are significant enough in the light of all that has been said here, perhaps, to be in the record."

Mr. Velde gave permission, and these points were subsequently filed in the final exhibit, as follows:

Summary of Impressions Following Visit to Russia, Summer 1934. From Diary Record of August 25, 1934.

1. I am impressed by the apparent fact that their political education has gone down. There is exceptional ability manifest by worker, by peasant, and young people in the discussion of political and economic matters. Like young fundamentalists, these people are saturated in Marx, know the answers in terms of Communist dogma, and are absolutely "certain" they are right and scientifically correct.

2. I am impressed by the fact that revolution was a much easier task here than it would be in the United States. Our middle classes have a standard of life these people never knew. Classes are not fixed in the U. S. Our leadership is infinitely abler. Our business men possess an efficiency and adaptability unknown to pre-revolution Russians.

3. I am impressed more and more by the treatment of minorities. They are gagged, at times starved. How can an opposition idea get under way, even if true? Here dogma comes in. Opposition ideas cannot be true. We have the truth.

4. I am impressed by the strange contradiction between the vast conceptions of social organization and the apparent advance and the extraordinary inefficiency in carrying out detail, in preventing waste, in developing sanitation, and a score of such matters. Those impressed by organizing skill as shown in Red Square parade must remember that is military, a machine, and does not call for individual initiative and decision, as well as care. Everything seems allowed to deteriorate.

5. I am impressed by the intellectual isolation of the people. This is a fundamental contradiction of so-called scientific spirit.

6. I am impressed by the need of Americans to See America First. People should know our own social work, our own schools, our own fac-

tories—and they would be less impressed by work that is distinctly
inferior but is held up in Russia as superior. These Russians assume
we are coming to find out how it is done.

7. I am impressed by the fact that a Communist state appropriates all
the lessons, the costly experiments, the trial and error learnings of
capitalism. Let us see later how much advance technically they will
themselves make.

8. I am impressed by the danger to the creative mind. He, if in opposition, is silenced, killed.

9. Art, to date, while we are told it is "flighting wings" has done prac-
tically nothing. Perhaps the new ideas will manifest themselves in
new concepts in art, but not yet.

10. I am impressed by the paralyzing consequences of bureaucracy, when
the order of the bureaucrat is in the hands of the ignorant, who
denied freedom to exercise creative judgment and reasonable adaptability, a person generally unimaginative, blocks the traffic of a great
arterial street, because the order he received said, "Traffic north and
south when green light burns; traffic stops when red light burns."
But signal got out of order. East and west must stand still until signal
is repaired or order rescinded.

Mr. Kunzig then stooped to what I regarded as both an undignified and well-nigh unforgivable stratagem. He introduced an article
that had been written by Miss Winifred Chappell in 1934.

First, he pointed out that Miss Chappell was a secretary of the
Methodist Federation for Social Service, that my name had appeared
on the same letterhead when we were celebrating the twentieth anniversary of the Federation. He wanted to know how long I had
known her.

I replied, "I simply met her."

Mr. Scherer broke in, "Did you know that Winifred Chappell
was a member of the Communist Party?"

Miss Chappell is dead. She was accused in an executive session of
this Committee of Party membership. She had never been heard. But
accusation from Mr. Scherer appears to be conviction.

Mr. Jackson wanted to know, "What was your capacity at the time Winifred Chappell was active in the Epworth League?"

I replied, "I was the pastor, I believe, of the Church of All Nations in Los Angeles."

Mr. Scherer asked, "Were you a member of the Methodist Federation at that time, Bishop?"

I testified that I was. Actually, I was one of some five thousand members. At the time Miss Chappell's statement came out, I was president of DePauw University.

The little skit had now reached its climax. Messrs. Clardy, Scherer and Kunzig stepped to the side and Mr. Jackson stood center stage, spotlighted. He read his lines well. "Are you familiar, sir, with a statement in the *Epworth Herald*, I believe, which was written by Winifred Chappell? I will read it to you—"

I replied, "You don't need to read it. I have read it, and I deplore it, and I do not know why these matters are constantly brought up in connection with me."

But Mr. Jackson was not to be denied his big moment. He said, "I am going to ask permission of the Committee to read it." Mr. Walter was heard from the wings, "I would like to hear it myself. You and the Bishop apparently know what it is, but the rest of us do not."

Mr. Velde had to speak his line. He said, "I am sure I do not." But Mr. Velde had told me that he himself had worked upon the report of the Committee on the Methodist Federation for Social Action, and that very statement had been included in that report. I tried to head Mr. Jackson off by saying, "She was advising somebody to avoid the draft, a deplorable thing to me."

But Mr. Jackson was insistent, and read the article. There could be but one purpose and that was to associate me with such views. When he finished, I said, "Mr. Chairman, if Mr. Jackson will state what he thinks of that, he and I will be in complete agreement, and I wish he would state it."

But Mr. Jackson was not to be trapped. He wanted to know if the *Epworth Herald* was an official publication of the Church, and inquired, "What action was taken either within the Methodist Federation or within the Methodist Church in the form of the disciplinary action relative to this statement?"

I replied, "I think none. We do not discipline people for statements, much as I deplore that. It should never have been there. She was not an editor—"

Mr. Moulder asked the proper question, "Were you in a position to exercise any control or authority over Miss Chappell?"

I replied, "None whatsoever."

It seemed to me these gentlemen were determined to portray me in the worst light. They knew perfectly well I had no sympathy for communism. They knew that I had never co-operated knowingly or willingly with Communists. In fact, they knew the direct reverse to be true.

Mr. Clardy suggested by implication that I must be sympathetic with the Methodist Federation which "by subtle means" praised the collectivist system. He spoke of "myriad examples," and that he was "utterly convinced that they were carrying out . . . the Communist Party line."

I tried to summarize my personal beliefs concerning the economic order. We were nearing the end of the hearing. The members of the Committee evidenced fatigue. I could have wished full opportunity to answer that query; I said, "You see, Mr. Chairman, I believe the American way has been, let us say, a dynamic way. We have never been pledged to what you may call dogmatism. We speak of our economic system. Now, just what is that system?"

Had there been time, I would have introduced the paragraph I had written for the great National Study Conference on the Church and Economic Life to which 382 delegates officially appointed by 22 denominations had come. I had been requested to write the message entitled "An Affirmation of Christian Concern and a Call to Action in Relation to Economic Life." After drafting the document with considerable care, it was submitted to a small committee for critical consideration. It was revised in the light of that criticism and read to the Conference. It was then referred to a committee composed of nineteen individuals, among them Noel Sargent, secretary of the National Association of Manufacturers; John L. Lovett, the general executive of the Manufacturers' Association of the State of Michigan; Dr. William Adams Brown, Jr., of Brookings Institution in Washington. It had been adopted with no substantial change and when read to the great Assembly was approved with but one dissenting vote. In it was a paragraph vital to this consideration, but time denied me the privilege of reading it.

Christians judge all economic systems by the imperatives of the Christian faith; Christians must not identify any economic order with the Gospel. The Christian Gospel is not to be found in Adam Smith's "Wealth of Nations" nor in Karl Marx's "Kapital." It is to be found in Matthew, Mark, Luke, and John, in the Acts of the Apostles, the Epistles of the New Testament, and the vision of St. John in the Revelation. It is to be found in the preaching of the Hebrew prophets, in the lives of saints and martyrs, in the service of the faithful followers of Christ, and in the continuing revelation of God. That faith affirms the supreme worth of persons. Institutions must be tested finally by their contribution to the enrichment of personality.

I said, "In the American system, for instance, we have a public highway system. I think it is the best in the world. It is collectively owned. I do not want somebody calling it socialist. I believe it is American, and it is good."

Mr. Walter asked, "The highway system is collectively owned?"

I answered, "The public highway system is owned by the people, yes, sir. We have a public school system which is owned by the people. I do not want it called socialism. I believe it is American, and it is good. I will not call the roll, but when I see the light-houses when I fly in here, and I know of that service, I am proud of those men.

It is true it is a governmental service, but I think it is American, and it is good. Run it all the way down until you come to the national parks.

"Now, personally, I believe it is better to have the national parks handled as they are handled than to have them privately owned and privately run."

Mr. Walter asked, "Mr. Chairman, what has this to do with the question?" Mr. Walter's interruption was followed by Mr. Clardy. I was determined not to be turned from answering this question. Had there been time, I would have spelled this out in detail, referring to the Departments of Agriculture and of Commerce, the Reclamation Service, and the Bureau of Standards. I would have said, in each case, that that work is American and it is good. I would have pointed out the Hoover Dam, and said, I am glad that it is owned by the people and that a fair allocation of the energy developed is made available both to private enterprise and to municipal and state enterprise. I would have declared, I think the Hoover Dam is American. I believe it is good.

I would have dealt then with the activities clothed with public interest that involve regulation, and would have said, eternal vigilance is the price of liberty here as elsewhere. The service of the Interstate Commerce Commission, the Security Exchange Commission, and similar regulatory bodies are a part of the American system. It is good. Surely the regulation of traffic is not regimentation. It is necessary. It is American and it is good.

I coveted the time to describe the development of American enterprise, the genius of American leadership, the building of the greatest productive machine upon the face of the earth. I did have opportunity to say, "Personally, I believe that in the overwhelming percentage of American enterprise, private enterprise in the long run will result in greater creativity, greater productivity and make a greater contribution to freedom than any system man has known."

I concluded by saying, "Now that is my position," and went on,

"To answer your question, sir: Professor Ward believed that the capitalist system was evil. He believed that there was a sinful principle at its heart. During the period up to 1932 that was not stressed over much. It did come to the fore from then on, and you recall that they even changed the masthead, the statement as to the objective of the Federation, until you could call it a socialist objective. I disagreed with that fundamentally. That was a part of this disagreement that I am talking about. Now, there was one answer there, either get out or try to change it. I did the best I could. I did not change it, and I am sorry. I left the organization when I stated, but I want my own position clearly understood here regarding what I believe to be the free way in the economic order."

But these men hung on tenaciously. Mr. Velde wanted to know if I had ever cast a vote for Jack McMichael as executive secretary. I replied, "I do not believe I ever did."

Mr. Clardy was unwilling to call it a day. He held up a volume that I had edited in 1933, *Preaching and the Social Crisis*. He did not explain that these were lectures delivered by several nationally prominent leaders at the Boston University Conference on Preaching, that my relationship to this volume had been that of editor. The young ministers had been eager to hear answers to the problems then confronting the nation. It was at the depth of the depression. Mr. Clardy tried to implicate Kirby Page in the Communist conspiracy. Kirby Page was an absolute pacifist, utterly opposed to the Communist philosophy and method. I do not see how any man could have misrepresented a volume more effectively than Mr. Clardy did. Mr. Velde broke in, stating, "I think we are getting to irrelevant material." He was right.

I replied to Mr. Clardy, "I wish, sir, you had read my introduction to that book."

He said, "I have, and do not misunderstand me: I am not accusing you of being a Communist or anything akin to it. Far from it, but I do think that you were muddled in your thinking and unclear in your understanding." Mr. Clardy stated he had read that book "in its entirety many times." I do not know what he means by many, but his statement would raise questions concerning his ability to pass a "comprehension test." After all that had been said concerning Professor Ward, Mr. Kunzig insisted upon placing in the record testimony of Manning Johnson delivered in executive session relative to Professor Ward. I was growing weary of this trickery, and finally asked, "Mr. Chairman, may I ask, I thought we were here to correct my files. This is all interesting information, and it seems to me places . . . an obligation upon this Committee to make it possible for those within the church who have authority to take action, . . . but why it is involved in my case, I find it a little hard to understand."

Mr. Jackson broke in implying that I should have known all about this. I answered, "Mr. Jackson, you didn't know anything about this until this testimony under subpoena came in. The church doesn't have the power to subpoena these former Communists. We cleared up that organization as far as the church is concerned. There is official action taken concerning the Methodist Federation for Social Action, and in 1936 I wrote the Resolution that called upon all agencies that are not regular agencies of the church, to put in their title the term 'unofficial.' I personally wrote that and through the years they always did that."

MR. JACKSON: "It is true we did not participate in this testimony until it was developed. We felt justified in issuing a report."

BISHOP OXNAM: "But your report came to no conclusion and anybody reading that report cannot tell what the opinion of the Committee is."

MR. JACKSON: "There has been evidence over a very long period of time that there were activities within the Methodist Federation for Social Action which appeared to be Communist-directed and now I may add, from what we had in the way of background material, we now have the sworn testimony which indicates that what was believed to be the case was indeed the case."

BISHOP OXNAM: "How can that be helpful to those of us in the church facing this kind of a situation?"

MR. JACKSON: "I think the Committee has been of great service in bringing forth the fact that the Methodist ministers, in one case as I understand your testimony, an active member, an active pastor at the present time is or has been a member of the Communist Party. I believe that unless this Committee had been functioning, unless this testimony had been taken, that matter might have gone on and on and on and have been unknown for all time to come."

BISHOP OXNAM: "Mr. Chairman, was Jack McMichael called before the Committee? Did he have any opportunity to answer that? I am not pleading for him, but did he have a chance to answer what was alleged?"

MR. VELDE: "As far as I am concerned, Mr. Jack McMichael has never been called before this Committee."

BISHOP OXNAM: "Then this is given to the public all over the nation before the man accused has had so much as an opportunity to answer."

MR. SCHERER: "Do you concur that Reverend McMichael is a member of the Communist Party today? You said so yourself."

I had said nothing of the kind, and answered, "That isn't correct at all."

MR. SCHERER: "On the basis of the testimony we had in New York, sworn testimony of any number of witnesses, and on that basis how could any reasonable person come to any other conclusion than that Dr. Ward and Reverend McMichael are dangerous Communists?"

BISHOP OXNAM: "That isn't it."

MR. SCHERER: "What is it?"

BISHOP OXNAM: "That a man is accused before a decision is reached, and I do not believe this is a court."

MR. VELDE: "This certainly is not a court, but what I am puzzled about, Bishop, you have your suspicions regarding these people, Dr.

Ward and Reverend McMichael, for some years. What did you do about it? It seems to me your obligation as an American citizen should be to report that to some investigative agency, whether it be this body or whether it be the Federal Bureau of Investigation, the ONI or G-2."

Had he forgotten so soon?

BISHOP OXNAM: "I told you I had discussed the question of Jack McMichael and I would be glad to tell the Committee with whom in executive session."

MR. VELDE: "Your confidence will be respected."

Mr. Scherer who had had little to say during the day referred to an article I had contributed to *Parade* magazine. "You say that the uncovering of Communists in religion should be left up to the clergy and now you admit . . . that you have been unable to cope with it in the Methodist Federation for Social Action, of which you were a part."

The *Parade* article had made no such statement, so I requested that it be included in the record, and this was done. Mr. Scherer's tone and facial expression suggested that he disbelieved me and therefore discounted any statement. He said, "I might call your attention to a speech or statement you made a few weeks ago when you challenged the Committee to prove that there was one Communist member of the clergy."

I replied, "I think I said to name any one Communist who held a position of major responsibility in any church."

Mr. Clardy had to keep in the act, and said, "Did you not say you didn't know any?"

I answered, "I made two statements. One was much earlier in which I said that I did not know of a Communist in the Methodist Church, and the second had to do with the Philadelphia speech . . . a great meeting of a good many thousand people, and I made reference to the fact that I would challenge anybody to name a Communist who held a position of major responsibility in any of our churches. I still haven't heard. There may be such a person. If so, I regret it."

Mr. Scherer asked, "How about Reverend McMichael?"

I replied, "We do not consider that McMichael had a large position. That is an unofficial position." The questions and answers that followed grew out of the continuing attempt of the Committee to impeach my public statements rather than to investigate un-American activities. I sought to introduce the study of the Committee that had been made by Professor Carr of Dartmouth, but when we got down to a discussion of procedures, Mr. Velde jumped in, saying, "Mr. Clardy, I think we are getting irrelevant."

Mr. Doyle confirmed the fact that the hearings in New York were preparatory to my hearing. He said, "This Committee had no knowledge as far as our record was concerned of the attitude of Dr. Ward or Reverend McMichael until, may I say, we were getting ready for this hearing. . . . It is a difficult matter to get evidence on Communists. It is not an easy thing, even for our expert investigators." He then said, "One further observation, Mr. Chairman, it is eleven o'clock. This witness has mentioned a dozen times, I think, that he wanted to have his record clear and identified and corrected, if it should be corrected, and I think before we take more time to prove who Dr. Ward was and who Reverend McMichael was, that the witness ought to understand when he leaves this room whether or not he has any corrections to make in his record. I understood that is why he came."

Mr. Velde broke in, "Mr. Doyle, I think this matter should be taken up in executive session."

Mr. Doyle asked, "What should be?"

Mr. Velde replied, "The matter of correction of any of the records."

Mr. Doyle added, "I thought the subject matter was the files of the Committee, and that is what I am interested in, getting that before we adjourn."

Mr. Clardy a moment later said, "To concentrate on something that you have said, you mentioned some criticism of the Committee procedure and I think that is very much in point and something that ought to be discussed. I want to ask this; didn't you, just a few minutes ago, suggest that because the church lacked what this Committee possesses, the power of subpoena, that you could not uncover these things that we were inquiring about?"

I answered, "Yes, sir; I did."

He went on, "With that in mind, would you not agree with us that because we do have the power of Congress, the power of subpoena and the power to investigate which the church does not, that we are far better equipped? I am not talking about files or anything else, but aren't we better equipped to do the job for you and for the nation as a whole?"

I said, "Mr. Chairman, I have always believed there is a proper place for Congressional investigations. It is a part of our American system. I have been dealing with what I believe to be an unfortunate handling of the files.

"Mr. Doyle has just made reference to the rules. I read them. I think anybody reading those rules will recognize distinct improvements."

It is possible that these men have been wounded by criticism and have not taken time to consider the criticism objectively. They have taken it personally. Mr. Clardy appeared unacquainted with the essential point I made, which had to do with the release of files to the public.

He asked, "Do you think that the procedure you are suggesting, do you think that would work in an investigation of a Communist? Don't you see that you would utterly, as you quoted me in *Parade*, utterly destroy the investigative process? I said that. I meant that, not only for that but for other reasons. We have sat here and taken abuse day after day and week after week and months after month and if you had gone through the fire and furnace that we have you would understand what we have gone through."

MR. VELDE: "Mr. Clardy, I think we are getting irrelevant."

MR. CLARDY: "I don't think so, Mr. Chairman."

MR. VELDE: "It is interesting."

MR. CLARDY: "Not only is it interesting but it is important. I want the record to show that it is in point because I believe that it is necessary to point out some of the misconceptions that the good witness possesses."

MR. VELDE: "Proceed."

Then Mr. Kunzig said, "I would like to offer into evidence Oxnam Exhibits 30, 31, 32, 33, 34, 35 and 36. They are all the documents we have been talking about for the last half hour but I haven't had a chance to put them into evidence until this moment."

They were introduced, the witness having had no opportunity to see them or to comment upon them.

◀ VIII ▶

I protest against the failure of the House Committee on Un-American Activities, after spending hundreds of thousands of dollars of tax funds, to propose sound legislation to end the communist menace or to suggest constructive proposals to remove the causes that produce communism or creative measures to make us impregnable to communist infiltration.

I RECALLED the improper assumptions upon which the Committee based its procedures.

In its publication *One Hundred Things You Should Know About Communism*, the Committee asks, "What is the best way to combat Communism?" The answer is: "Detection, exposure, and prosecution." Has the Committee never heard of preventive measures? Is the

Committee set up to be a superdetective agency? Or is the duty of detection a proper obligation of the Federal Bureau of Investigation?

One of the many failings of the Committee is not to make use of the great resources available in the fight against communism. There are many men in the nation who have studied communism, who understand its philosophy, are aware of its unscientific theory of social development, are acquainted with the fallacies of its economics, and are alert to its freedom-destroying insistence upon dictatorship. There are others who have made careful psychological studies, and are in a position to testify concerning the factors that turn youth to the Communist conspiracy. Has the Committee sought the judgment of great labor leaders like George Meaney and Walter Reuther? Has it conferred with Morris Ernst and considered the Report on the American Communist which he and David Loth drafted? What does the Committee recommend when facing the fact that most people join the Communist Party between the ages of eighteen and twenty-three? Are the measures proposed by this Committee, if any, designed to make it easier for people to leave the conspiracy? Or do the procedures of the Committee drive disillusioned Communists into hiding? Is the Committee aware of the fact that members of the Party do not come from poverty-stricken homes, but have been reared in comfort? What is it that attracts them? Can these attractions be dissipated? Mr. Ernst notes the striking fact of an extremely high incidence of suicides, desertions and divorces among the parents, brothers and sisters, or close relatives of those who join the party. Has the Committee given any indication that it is aware of the social factors that contribute to the making of Communists? Does it know that these young people, as a rule, do not join the Party for personal gain or for power? They believe they are entering an effective campaign against war, poverty and discrimination, and that communism offers a scientific answer to these questions. Is the impact of the Committee on education of such a nature that teachers are afraid to examine the nature of communism and to expose it for what it is? This is exposure that might be effective.

Does the Committee know that psychologically these young people are often cursed by a sense of personal inadequacy, that they lack humor and optimism? That the bulk of the membership is in the larger cities, and the rank and file almost entirely native-born and white? True enough, the leadership has many more foreign-born within it, and the top command is in reality, if not in fact, Russian. The professional leaders are cynical, determined, ruthless, and act without scruple. What is the significance of the fact that most of the young people who enter the movement have already lost religious faith? What is the Committee's answer to the tremendous fact that, according to the best estimates, 700,000 men and women have left the Communist Party in this country in the last thirty years?

If the Committee would give some attention to such studies and come up with practical proposals and follow procedures in accordance with American tradition, praise would supplant criticism, and together the threat might be faced and the movement defeated.

But the Committee thinks in terms of detection, not prevention. It calls for exposure, and this may be a proper function for an investigating committee. Some committees have rendered signal service by exposing corrupt practices, such as in the Teapot Dome scandals. But exposure involves careful investigation. It becomes indecent exposure when decent citizens are stripped and paraded before eager eyes and drooling mouths to make Roman Holiday for a politician whose objective is office rather than truth.

Has the Committee published a single competent study upon the Communist method? Has it solicited the co-operation of philosophers qualified to answer a philosophy of materialism? It has sought to expose persons. It should expose an ideology, also.

In the contemporary scene, the free society is confronted by an expanding imperialism, which is Soviet Russia, and by an infiltrating ideology, which is Soviet communism. I am one who believes that the nation must be so strong as to convince the Soviet imperialist that further to expand will jeopardize the peace, and having jeopardized it, he cannot, because of our strength, win. On the other hand, it must be evident to thoughtful men that an ideology cannot be demolished by atomic bombs. It must be met by a better ideology, equally dynamic, one that when translated into actuality brings more of abundant living to men.

If we would preserve the free society, we must face the issues of power and of justice. Power must be brought under democratic control, all kinds of power, political power, economic power, ecclesiastical power. Justice must be established by the democratic process.

What has the Committee done to summon men to an intelligent attack upon the ideology? Little, or nothing. It has relied too largely upon the help of former Communists. They may be sincere. Christianity believes in conversion; and some of these men may be changed. It is nevertheless true that no Communist could want a committee to follow a course that differs from that of the present Committee, as it centers its attention on effects, fails to deal with causes, spreads fear and rumor, divides the American people, sets neighbor against neighbor, and drives trust from our midst.

If the Communists are as clever as some allege, an admission I am unwilling to make, they might well have set such persons in such positions of influence to contribute the very incompetency against which I protest.

The Committee conceives its work as detection and as exposure. In using the term "prosecution" does it think of itself as having supplanted the courts? Perhaps not; but its procedures are in effect prosecution. The Committee is not charged with this duty. Not a few members of investigating committees have used expressions to indicate that they thought of themselves as members of a court. They act like a court, without obeying the restrictions that law puts upon court procedure. They seek to be judge, jury and hangman. Members have boasted that they have been instrumental in separating men from their jobs. Thus they steal a man's livelihood. The private lists of "controversial persons" become an effective blacklist, and artists no longer sing, act or entertain.

Detection! Exposure! Prosecution!

When the Bishops of the Methodist Church faced this issue, they said:

We reject Communism, its materialism, its method of class war, its use of dictatorship, its fallacious economics, and its false theory of social development; but we know that the only way to defeat it permanently is to use the freedom of our own democracy to establish economic justice and racial brotherhood. It is the man who is not exploited who is deaf to the slogan, "Abolish the exploitation of man by man." It is the man who knows he is treated justly who refuses the sinister suggestion of revolutionary activity to win justice. The most effective anti-toxin to dictatorship abroad is life-giving democracy at home. It is a healthy democracy that is immune to Communist bacteria. . . . The most certain way to destroy dictatorship abroad is to establish democracy at home. Liberty, equality, and fraternity are contagious; and if present in sufficient vitality, may become epidemic. Let people who suffer dictatorship behold a nation in which man has preserved his liberty, established equality, and practices fraternity, and it is certain as day follows night that such vision will become a revolutionary force that will not rest until freedom is won. Socially controllable inequalities must be removed. Justice and brotherhood within the conditions of freedom are like bells. They sound the death knell of Communism. Communism will never win a democratic and just America. Communism does not grow in the soil of freedom and justice. It takes root in the soil of exploitation. It is democracy—more of it, not less of it—that will win the morrow.

Has anyone studied the record of the majority members of the Committee in labor legislation? What have these men stood for in social reform?

All of this is so distinctly personal that I feel free to indicate that I wrote the Episcopal Address, signed by all of the Bishops of the

Methodist Church, from which the quotation concerning communism came. This was never included in the files.

The fact that I had written the resolution putting the Methodist Church on record as opposed to communism in 1936 is not in the files.

Nor was the clear condemnation of communism that is found in every book I have written from 1927 to the present in files that were supposed to give "the philosophical bent" of an individual.

No wonder an honest man protests!

We were approaching the midnight hour. I was prepared to sit there until morning, if it were necessary. I recalled the words of our old football coach. Between halves he used to say, "Just remember, they are as tired as you are."

A Committee that had been requested to consider falsehoods and misleading statements which it had released over a period of many years continued to introduce material that had not been in the releases. Mr. Kunzig to reassure us said, "There are a few other things." He then quoted what was at that time designated as Exhibit No. 38, a letter that had been sent by the Division of Foreign Missions of the Methodist Church to the ministers of the Church. Mr. Kunzig had become expert in introducing an exhibit. His craftiness was less subtle than he may have imagined. He said, "I believe you sent a letter to 'Dear Fellow Workers' of the Board of Missions and Church Extension of the Methodist Church, in which you sent out a book. Since you have discussed this fairly recently, I think you know the book to which I am referring. It is *Behind Soviet Power*, by Jerome Davis, who of course is an identified Communist."

The use of the words "of course," the tone of voice, withholding the fact that the letter had been sent by the Division of Foreign Missions itself, the identification of Dr. Davis as an "identified Communist" were all a part of the byplay that lay in the question itself.

I interrupted, "Just a moment, is that true? I believe that the *Saturday Evening Post* paid Mr. Davis $15,000 for calling him a

Communist. I don't want anybody to think that I was sending out or related to the sending out of a book of a Communist."

Mr. Jackson's face revealed concern. He said, "I think if there is any reason for a binding impression, in view of the statement of the witness, that that portion should be stricken from the record which suggests—and I may be in error but I think pending a personal check which I would prefer to make myself, that that portion of counsel's statement which deals with the identification be stricken from the record."

MR. VELDE: "Without objection, that part will be stricken from the record."

BISHOP OXNAM: "Which statement, Mr. Chairman?"

MR. VELDE: "The statement and question of counsel."

BISHOP OXNAM: "Thank you, sir."

With what ease these men bandy about the term "Communist." When they are confronted by the fact that a great paper had been sued and had to pay for its libel, the Committee runs to cover. Then Mr. Kunzig insisted upon introducing into the record ten or eleven pages of the so-called Front record of Jerome Davis.

Mr. Frazier asked, "May I inquire as to the pertinency of the introduction of that particular article?"

And Mr. Doyle said, "I would like to raise this point; if it is material that the first question and the answer with reference to Mr. Davis be stricken, might it not be well to keep this out of the record until someone checks to know what the fact is?"

Mr. Clardy insisted that two witnesses had identified Jerome Davis. He did not say as what. It was assumed that he meant identified as a Communist. Some debate followed, but at last they voted to include it.

Here the Committee clearly invaded the field of religion. This book had been sent to Methodist ministers by order of the Administrative Committee of the Board of Missions and Church Extension of the Methodist Church. It was an official action of one of the great official agencies of the largest Protestant denomination in America. I had signed the letter that accompanied the book because I was president of the Division. So far as I know, this is the first time in American history that any investigating committee had presumed to question the right of the Church to send such literature to its ministers as it deemed wise. The purpose that lay behind the decision of the Administrative Committee was clearly stated in the letter that accompanied the book. "There is a moral obligation to become acquainted with the facts involved in our present relationship with Russia." The letter stated that "the rapid spread of Russian influence throughout the world is a most significant challenge to the World Mission of Christ."

Dr. Ralph E. Diffendorfer, the executive secretary of the Division of Foreign Missions of the Methodist Church, one of the most distinguished missionary leaders of the generation, commented upon this sentence, saying, "The word 'challenge' is well known in the missionary world, and it is always used to indicate a force which Christianity must take into account and never indicates propaganda on behalf of any point of view. For instance, if one used the statement that 'Pan Islam is the greatest challenge to Christianity in the Middle East, Southern and Southwestern Asia,' no one would ever think that the user of that sentence was advocating the merits of Islam. The meaning is quite the contrary." The letter stated that this book "should be read in conjunction with other authoritative volumes, particularly, in connection with the Federal Council of the Churches of Christ's statement referred to above, as well as with Vera Micheles Dean's discussion in the July-August 1946 Headline Series of the Foreign Policy Association, entitled 'Russia—Menace or Promise?' "

The volume sent out by the Division of Foreign Missions of the Methodist Church carried the endorsement of Dr. John R. Mott, winner of the Nobel prize for peace and generally regarded as the outstanding Christian layman of our day. He said, "Necessary, timely, fair-minded, should be read by all." Grove Patterson, editor-in-chief of the *Toledo Blade,* commended it, saying, "More sound information about the Soviet Union than I have found in all the books and pamphlets I have read." Daniel A. Poling, whose vigorous anti-communism is internationally known, was quoted as commending the book in these words, "The most challenging, at the same time, the most objective study on Russia." Among others commending the book, whose commendations appear on the back cover, was Raymond Robbins, who commanded the American Red Cross mission to Russia and who is described as an unofficial agent of the United States government during the first seven months of the Soviet regime. He said, "Dr. Jerome Davis knew Russia under the Czars, under Kerensky, and under Lenin and Stalin. He speaks the language of the Russian people. All that he writes on the Soviet Union is supported by first hand and competent investigation. He has always been concerned about the facts and let theories take care of themselves."

I should have informed this Committee that this matter was none of its business. I did not wish to irritate them at the close of a hearing. I still hoped that we might consider the files and that we might get some kind of correction.

Mr. Kunzig asked, "Did you send that book to the Methodist ministers throughout the country?"

I replied, "If you will rephrase that question, I will answer it in the affirmative. When you ask 'Did you send it?,' I did not. This was sent by the order of the Administrative Committee of the Board of Missions and Church Extension of the Methodist Church. . . . It was actually sent by the Board itself. I must take responsibility as I was president of the Board and did sign the letter, but when you use the term 'you sent it,' I have to say it was sent by the Board of Missions and Church Extension of the Methodist Church."

Mr. Velde then wanted to know the composition of the Committee. Once again, it was none of the business of a committee such as this. Here was a clear crossing of the line that separates church and state. Here was an invasion in fact of the realm which Mr. Velde had vehemently stated he had no intention of entering.

Mr. Jackson pressed the matter even further and asked, "Which individual selected the book, or was it a matter of a subcommittee selection?"

I replied, "Dr. Ralph E. Diffendorfer, who was the executive secretary of the Division of Foreign Missions, a gentleman who was responsible for founding the International Christian University in Japan, generally regarded as one of the ablest missionaries of the last generation, and who is dead now, said he thought it would be well for our people to understand the challenge to our faith that lies in the whole Communist movement. He felt this book would make a contribution to it. Methodist ministers know how to read books and can read critically. I said that I thought if this book went out it ought to be accompanied by the statement . . . that was issued by the Federal Council of the Churches of Christ in America on American-Soviet relations. I had chaired that committee that had drafted this statement. It is no secret, however, that it was written by John Foster Dulles. We went over it sentence by sentence. Very few changes were made or are ever made in anything that Mr. Dulles drafts because he is extraordinarily effective in those matters. That particular statement contains one of the severest condemnations of communism that I think you will find. It is an intellectual condemnation of communism."

Mr. Clardy made reference to Mrs. Dean's book. I had said "that we regarded that as an excellent factual presentation of a situation by a competent scholar, and I would repeat that, sir."

He then said, "And I have read it and I have extensive notes and I regard it as one of the most arrogant pro-Communist statements that I have been privileged to read."

This was pompous nonsense which I fear elicited a sharp reply. I said, "You are expressing your judgment and it differs from the judgment of some of the people, qualified people in this nation on foreign issues and the Foreign Policy Association." I turned to the Chairman and said, "May I ask, Mr. Chairman, what is the point of that?"

Mr. Velde ignored me and said, "Counsel will proceed."

Some by-play followed, in which Mr. Jackson requested the date when the National Council of American-Soviet Friendship had been cited, and the date when Mrs. Dean's book had been recommended in a bibliography issued by the Council. It was all very clear, not to say stupid. I knew these gentlemen were speaking for the record. I knew that we were within a few minutes of adjournment, and so I said, "It should be pointed out that at this particular time the Secretary of State of the United States of America, in the eighteen months of his service, traveled some 70,000 miles for the purpose of maintaining what was called the Grand Alliance of the Great War, trying to keep together the permanent members of the Security Council. At this very time that was what was being done by the Government of the United States of America. I could defend this book upon an entirely different basis. I do not want to do it because our purpose was not that. Our purpose was, frankly, to acquaint our people with the challenge that does lie in communism to our faith, but this matter of not noting dates and of referring to a book that appears in somebody else's bibliography, really it doesn't become us."

Mr. Clardy launched into additional criticism of Mrs. Dean's book. Mr. Doyle said, "I want to make this one further remark, and I believe it is pertinent. You have given the other members the chance to discuss books. I think from my personal experience we have had plenty of talk about book burning in Washington and I hope that no member of this Committee is getting into a mental attitude of where we are going to think in terms of book burning or book destruction. I think it is very unfortunate that this kind of question should arise."

I had thought the hearing was over. To my amazement, Mr.

Kunzig took a fresh start. He asked, "Do you know Reverend Stephen H. Fritchman?"

I stated that I had lectured at the First Unitarian Church where he is pastor, that I had always hoped there might be the best of relationships between the Unitarian and the Trinitarian Churches of the country. I did state that two prominent officials of the Unitarian Church had given me information that raised grave doubts concerning Dr. Fritchman, and that if I had had that information before lecturing in Los Angeles in his church, I would not have accepted the invitation.

Mr. Jackson pointed out that Dr. Fritchman had been closely associated with the Communist Party or Communist-front organizations over a number of years, that he declined to answer questions as to his membership in the Communist Party on the grounds of the Fifth Amendment. I wrote Dr. Fritchman and received a letter stating that he had once appeared before the Committee and had stated under oath that he was not and had not been a member of the Communist Party. He refused to testify subsequently on the ground that it was none of the Committee's business to question his activities as a minister.

Mr. Frazier, no doubt fearful, as I was, that this might go on and on, and that we would never come to the files, said, "I suggest that the Bishop be allowed to deal with the questions that he came here to answer. His counsel will have to leave in a very few minutes."

Mr. Clardy and Mr. Velde were of the opinion that I had had opportunity to do just this. The record is clear enough. I replied, "Mr. Chairman, . . . I listed certain items that have not been considered here at all and which illustrate the method of the files that I think is objectionable."

Mr. Jackson also tried to make it appear that all of the items had been considered. I said, "I wonder if I could run down the list very briefly and close the matter. I have been here all day hoping that one might deal with some of these items, and it is getting toward midnight. I am tired and so are you."

Mr. Velde said, "I can see no further reason why we should go into this in this manner. . . . So I say that I think we have been more than fair in recognizing your objections to the file of this Committee and I ask, therefore, that we proceed in regular order and ask that counsel will ask any further questions that he might have."

Mr. Doyle objected to the ruling, stating, "If this witness feels he has a material point in connection with the files concerning him and which has not been presented yet and that is why we are here, I request that this witness have the opportunity to present any material point involved in the files which has not been presented, either by our counsel or by him. That was the purpose of this meeting. I think you ought to reconsider your ruling, Mr. Chairman."

Mr. Velde relented a little and asked, "How long will that take, Bishop?"

I replied, "I will take but one instance and I think I can do it in three minutes, if you will allow me to do it."

It was now clear I could not propose reform nor consider the file as I had requested.

I recalled Mr. Jackson's declaration that to criticize the procedures of investigating committees is to evidence sympathy for communism.

On the contrary, to demand the abrogation of police-state procedures is public testimony to Americanism.

I knew that on July 7, 1953, Congressman Dies, the former chairman of this Committee, introduced a resolution in the House. Its preamble noted "a bitter controversy between certain clergymen and educators, on the one hand, and certain committees of Congress investigating communism on the other" and declared, "Such committees are the agents of Congress for whose conduct and acts Congress is responsible." It provides that "no person, organization, or group, shall be accused publicly of communism or communist sympathy by any committee of Congress or sub-committee thereof or any member thereof, purporting to speak for such committee or sub-committee until a majority of the committee or sub-committee in executive session shall have reviewed the evidence . . . and shall have decided by majority vote that there is sufficient evidence of guilt to justify such public discussion."

He provides, further, that citizens shall not be questioned until, by majority vote, the Committee decides there "is sufficient evidence of guilt to justify such questioning." The resolution denies the chairman of a committee the right to issue any public statement with respect to the planned intentions or procedures of the committee, unless authorized by majority vote.

Mr. Dies appears to be confused as to the purpose of Congressional investigation and seems to think of the Committee as a court. His resolution provides, "No finding of guilt shall be based on hearsay evidence or suspicion. The evidence as a whole must be sufficient to convince reasonable minds of the guilt of such person, organization, or group before any finding of guilt shall be authorized."

The important matter is not to point out that Mr. Dies misconceives the purpose of Congressional investigation, but to note that he recognizes the abuses in procedure and the necessity for reform.

On March 19, 1953, Congressman Javits introduced a bill which calls upon the Committee on Rules of the House to exercise "continuous watchfulness" on the activities of such committees. He, too, provides that "no major investigations will be initiated without the approval of the majority of the committee . . . that every witness shall have an opportunity at the conclusion of his examination . . . to supplement . . . testimony . . . by making a brief written or oral statement which shall become a part of the record." He continues, "Any person who has been identified by name in a public session and who has reasonable grounds to believe that the testimony . . . tends to affect his reputation adversely . . . may file . . . a sworn statement of reasonable length concerning such testimony . . . or appear personally before the committee and testify in his own behalf, unless the committee by a majority vote shall determine otherwise." A very important provision gives a person who believes testimony has hurt him the right to submit written questions which may be asked such witnesses by members of the Committee. He may even call a reasonable number of witnesses in his own behalf.

Mr. Javits then comes to the fundamental question at issue in my hearing. His bill provides, "No committee shall circulate on its letterhead or over the signature of its members or its employees charges against individuals or organizations, except as the committee by a majority vote shall so determine."

Had this provision been law, and had it been observed by the Committee, I would never have been subjected to seven years of irresponsible "releases" which did adversely affect my reputation.

The fact that such bills are before the House ought to convince reasonable men that these committees have abused their privileges. They can no longer hide behind the allegation that "to criticize is to co-operate with the Communists."

The American people never authorized Congressional committees to construct a modern counterpart of the ancient bed of Procrustes. This bed, it will be remembered, was of a certain length. The victim was thrown upon it, and if he were too long, his legs were cut off to fit the bed length; and if he were too short, he was stretched to meet the required length.

Representatives who suffer from the Procrustean complex should be given psychiatric treatment at public expense.

◀ IX ▶

I protest against the constant use of the phrase "It is cited" without informing the public that most citations are not conclusions reached after careful research and confirmed by responsible bodies, but in the case of this Committee and of many State Committees are often the result of incompetent study, the collection of unverified rumor and staff listing. The use of the phrase "It is cited" is a device designed to discredit. It is sheer duplicity and is subject to the severest condemnation.

CONGRESSMAN KEATING, an objective and experienced committeeman, who has demonstrated in the conduct of hearings both the American spirit and the procedure essential to successful inquiry, introduced a bill on January 3, 1953. It is somewhat briefer than Mr. Javits' bill, but seeks to give similar protection. Mr. Keating comes to the heart of the matter when, in Section V, he proposes, "Any person who is specifically identified by name in a public hearing before any committee and who believes that testimony or other evidence given at such hearing or comment made by any member of the committee or its counsel tends to defame him or otherwise adversely affect his reputation, shall be afforded the following privileges: he may file with the committee a sworn statement, he may appear personally before the committee to testify in his own behalf, and, unless the committee by a majority vote shall determine otherwise, he has the right to call upon the committee to secure the appearance of witnesses whose testimony adversely affected him, and to cross-examine such witnesses, either personally or by counsel; but such cross-examination shall be limited to one hour as to any witness, unless the committee votes to lengthen the period. He shall also have the right to call witnesses in his own behalf."

On July 15, 1953, the House Committee on Un-American Activities published its own rules. Article X of its rules states that "where practicable, any person named in a public hearing before the Committee as subversive, fascist, communist, or affiliated with one or more subversive front organizations shall within a reasonable time be notified by registered letter." This rule has been disregarded by the Committee. I made inquiry concerning individuals named in the executive hearings in New York in early July, and learned that they had not received such notification. The Committee has definitely decided not to allow cross-examination. It insists that "a Congressional committee conducts a search for information, not a trial." The rules now call for a majority vote for the release of Committee reports.

On August 4, 1953, Congressman Doyle, testifying before the House Rules Sub-Committee, pointed out that the new rules also state, "Credibility of a witness testifying before the Committee in closed session, or furnishing the Committee information, claiming that a person is subversive, shall first be established by the Committee 'as far as practicable' before such testimony or information 'is released or made public in any manner.' "

On May 5, 1953, the American Civil Liberties Union addressed an important communication to Mr. Velde which pointed out that "the Subversive Activities Control Board, established by the Internal Security Act of 1950, has after lengthy hearings already determined the Communist Party to be a foreign-dominated revolutionary movement.

"No further testimony from or about individuals is needed for this purpose."

This significant statement raises the fundamental issue: is the

Committee to continue its feverish activities in order to demonstrate something that has already been determined?

The communication further states: "Moreover, that Act itself specifically disclaims any intention of outlawing the Party, as such, even with such determination of its nature; and even an acknowledged or proved present member of the Party is not, merely by being a member, violating the law." Consequently, the communication demands that "any evidence of illegal acts which may be revealed should be immediately and fully and vigorously acted upon by the Department of Justice."

The American Civil Liberties Union then declared that "exposure of Communist connections, where discontinued in good faith, unjustly damages reputation and professional standing."

In a personal and informal conference with Mr. Velde, he requested that I propose such reforms as I deemed necessary. Under date of May 5, 1953, I sent Mr. Velde the following recommendations:

1. There should be eliminated from every file the listing of and reference to affiliation with any organization which has not been declared subversive by a properly authorized agency of the Federal government.
2. In the case of alleged affiliation with an organization which has been declared subversive,
   (a) evidence of membership in the organization, beyond newspaper quotations and listing on letterheads, should be clearly established with respect to the individual involved, and
   (b) in case membership is so established, it should be listed in the file only if the membership has been voluntary and active after a date when the subversive character of the organization was declared, such "cut-off date" to be determined by the Committee with respect to each specific organization.
3. An individual on whom a file is compiled should have the right to review such a file, to submit his own evidence and testimony, and to enter any disclaimer or other information he may desire. In case evidence from a file is released, such testimony and information as is

provided by the individual concerned should be included in the evidence.

4. Committee files should be open only to Committee members and other members of the legislative body and to the individual involved, unless the materials therein have been reviewed, investigated, and properly substantiated, in which case they may be released upon a majority vote of the Committee.

Mr. Clardy rushed to the press, and declared that my recommendations would "destroy the entire investigative process." He did not say how.

In response to my assurance that I could give an instance of file misrepresentation in three minutes, Mr. Velde agreed.

I then quoted from a Committee release which I said indicated incompetency or slanted selection. The official release on official letterhead which the former Chairman of the Committee himself had enclosed in a letter to me, stated,

The Washington *Star* of February 10, 1930 carries a news item datelined Indiana State Reformatory, February 9th.

The article refers to a speech made by Dr. G. Bromley Oxnam, president of DePauw University, to the inmates of the reformatory. Dr. Oxnam is reported as decrying the practices of nations in entering into secret treatises and declaring that the slogan of the "America First" must be interpreted as meaning "America first in world service" and not "to be the first to go into Mexico to steal lands."

Mr. Velde asked, "Was that a quotation from a newspaper?"

I replied, "This was the Washington *Star* of February 10." Mr. Velde sought to justify the action of the Committee by stating that if it had appeared in the Washington *Star,* the Committee was doing me no harm to quote what had appeared.

This is a fundamental point. Someone must exercise judgment in the matter of selection. I have accused the research staff of slanted selection. There was available in the press a full statement, which, if it had been selected, would have given an entirely different impression because it was an actual account of what I actually said.

I went on to say, "Now I read to you what did appear in the Indianapolis *Star* of February 13, 1930. This was available to your research staff:

"The words referred to were taken from two different sections of the speech and combined by the reporter. I stated that one of the causes of war was selfish nationalism. I said, 'There is a right kind of nationalism. It is the nationalism that manifests itself in such love of country that one is willing to give all he possesses, his life if need be, to lift the life standards of his people. It is the kind of nationalism one feels when singing "America" with its poignant line "Land where my fathers died." '

"I interject this statement that since my father's death I could understand the meaning of that splendid line.

"It is the kind of nationalism one feels when he looks upon the towering skyline of New York when returning from Europe and knows that that is his country, not a Shylockian people bent upon grasping gold, but after all a people of idealism. There is a right kind of nationalism.

"But there is a wrong kind, and that is selfish nationalism. It is revealed in the slogan 'Germany Over All,' 'Britannia Rules the Waves,' 'Ourselves Alone,' or 'America First.' If we mean by 'America First,' America first in world service, it is a sublime slogan, but if we mean America first and because our oil reserves may some day be depleted we will allow certain groups to stir up public opinion that we will enter Mexico and steal her oil reserves because we need them, then that slogan will do for us just what it did for Germany a short time ago."

I concluded by saying, "Now, I suggest to you, sir, these two quotations say two fundamentally different things."

Mr. Velde tried to justify this practice. I sought to show him how ridiculous his contention was, by stating, "Mr. Jackson recommended to the American people that they read Jerome Davis' book." His exact words were, "I would suggest to every American listening to this program that they make an effort to obtain Jerome Davis' book, *Behind Soviet Power.*" That is what he actually said. Such a sentence taken out of its context does Mr. Jackson injustice.

Actually, he had referred to it as "one of the greatest apologies for Soviet aggression, I have ever read," and added, "I feel it is in effect actually Soviet propaganda today." It is hard to tell from Mr. Jackson's statements whether he had read the book. The point here is, that selecting a sentence that did appear in the press and quoting it without regard to context would be unfair to Mr. Jackson. It is just this that the Committee is doing as anyone who reads the two statements will see.

It would have been most embarrassing to have read Mr. Clardy's letters written to a Methodist minister in the light of letters written by a counsel of the Committee. There was no time to do this.

It is only fair to say that Mr. Velde finally said, "As I say, I would like to get out of here myself, but if you do have any objections, regardless of the time, will you do it?"

I countered with this suggestion. "Would you let me send a communication to the Committee?" The point was to send to the Committee what I had hoped I might file throughout the day. Mr. Velde wanted to know if I and others were satisfied. I said, "I will say I am satisfied at this hour. I would have much preferred to have gone down the line earlier but I cannot trespass upon this Committee forever. You gentlemen have duties tomorrow. You have said I might send a letter, and under those circumstances I am satisfied."

Surely, I thought this must be the end. Mr. Kunzig had his orders. He then said, "I have a document called 'An American Churchman in the Soviet Union' by the Reverend Louie D. Newton, president of the Southern Baptist Convention. This is a publication of the American Russian Institute, which is cited by Attorney General Clark in 1949 as communist." He stated that I had written the introduction to the booklet.

That was true. I said, "Dr. Louie D. Newton is one of the most distinguished ministers of the Baptist Church. He was the president of the Southern Baptist Convention. Dr. Newton went to Russia. I have been related to the National Council. We have always hoped that some day our Southern Baptist brethren might be in the National Council. Dr. Newton is a dear, personal friend. When he returned from Russia, he asked me if I would write an introduction to a booklet he was bringing out describing his visit. I would suggest the Committee read it. I would like it introduced. I had no knowledge of what organization was to publish it. When it came out, I noticed it was put out by this agency. I have no relation to that. I wrote an introduction to a booklet written by a friend, a distinguished clergyman."

Mr. Clardy wanted to know the date. I stated that I could not remember the date. He said, "His information was that it was 1952," and added that he could not state that positively. I told him that I thought that was not correct. I suppose the purpose was to indicate that I had written an article after an agency had been cited by the Attorney General. I looked it up after the hearing and found that the year was 1946.

Then came a question as to whether or no Dr. William E. B. DuBois, the Negro leader, had spoken at the Church of All Nations in Los Angeles in 1927. I had no recollection of that. Mr. Kunzig withdrew it. Apparently, he was getting tired, too.

I told Mr. Velde that I was leaving for Europe shortly and that I feared it would be impossible for me to get the exhibits in his hands before leaving and said I hoped it would not be considered a discourtesy. Mr. Velde replied, "I am sure the Committee will wish you Godspeed upon your journey."

Mr. Jackson could not leave it that way, however, and insisted that "we interpose the citations in each instance of the various organizations."

I asked, "Does this include organizations to which I do not belong?"

Mr. Jackson replied, "My motion deals with the organizations upon which you have been questioned and in which there are exhibits."

Mr. Doyle objected, but withdrew his objections after being sure that the date of the citation would appear. Mr. Doyle then called attention to an important matter. He said, "I think it has been very unfortunate. . . . A lot of organizations have been referred to which, only by inference, could this witness be entitled to have any connection with, even indirectly. I was hoping that it would not be printed and go out in the United States. It will be taken inferentially and we all know that it will. Those people will not read the fact that he was never a member of it, and the fact that his name was identified with it will be enough for them and the fact that he has testified he was not a member of it, and we have no evidence that he was a member—I think that is the damnable part of it. I use that language because I feel just that way about it."

Mr. Doyle wanted the record to show, at the place where any organization was mentioned that I had denied membership. He was aware of what has been done by private agencies in these matters. He sought to justify his recommendation by saying, "If that page is torn out and used by some sneak thief we cannot help it, but I believe the Bishop is entitled to that protection."

Mr. Clardy said, "May I ask the Bishop a question? You have been here all day and haven't you heard us make it abundantly clear what we think about that, and aren't you satisfied with what we have said?"

This had to do with whether or not I was directly or indirectly related to the Communist Party. I said, "I don't know if this Committee has learned how its documents are misused by organizations that deliberately seek to destroy one's character and it seems to me that protection of that kind should be given." I was referring to Mr. Doyle's proposal to insert that I had denied membership at the time the organization was referred to.

Mr. Doyle climaxed the session by making a formal motion. He said, "I move that the record show in these hearings that this Committee has no record of any Communist Party affiliation or membership by Bishop Oxnam."

To my utter amazement, I heard Mr. Jackson say, "I second the motion."

The record does not indicate what went on in the next few seconds. Mr. Velde appeared stunned. He finally stammered out, "Is there any objection to the motion of the gentleman from California?" He paused, and I thought perhaps Mr. Jackson might come to and realize how significant his second had been. He did not, and Mr. Velde said, "If not, the motion is carried."

Mr. Doyle pressed the matter further, and said, "I make the further motion that after every listing of the Bishop's name in any group which we have discussed today that it be clearly printed wherever the Bishop has denied membership that he did deny membership, and let the record stand on that so that any person reading the list of names in this publication . . . will see it right before him that the Bishop said he was never a member of that organization. We cannot do less. That is what the Bishop testified to. Why not let the people know what he testified to?"

Mr. Jackson had come to. He opposed this strenuously. He insisted that the record itself would tell the story. Mr. Doyle, who has sat through many of these hearings and understands the situation thoroughly, said, "My distinguished colleague from California well knows that . . . some pages . . . in the testimony of this witness that he was not a member of this organization or that one . . . will never be read by the people. They will read portions, and they will never read his testimony that he was not a member. Consequently, the Bishop will again be done a rank injustice. I see no harm. It would not cost us any more money to say that Bishop Oxnam was not a member of that organization." Mr. Clardy also objected. It was a re-enactment of the ancient double play, Tinker to Evers to Chance, only instead of occurring on the baseball diamond, it was in a committee room, and the players were Jackson to Clardy to Velde.

The hearing was about to adjourn. Mr. Jackson's opposition to

Mr. Doyle's motion prevailed and Mr. Velde announced, "The motion is defeated."

I tried to leave the hearing room in a pleasant mood, and am a little fearful that I went too far in courtesy. I said, "I would like to thank you personally for your courtesy throughout the day. I know at times I have talked at length. At no time have you rapped the gavel, and I appreciate that very much."

Mr. Velde replied, "I hope you appreciate that the chairman has a duty which is not always easy, not only to the members of the Committee but to the Congress and the country as well."

I replied, "Yes, sir, I do appreciate that."

He said, "I want to say to the witness that the members of the Committee appreciate the manner of ironing this matter out and as I have stated before if you have further information about any of these matters the Committee will appreciate hearing it."

I answered, "Thank you very much."

Mr. Velde announced, "The Committee will stand adjourned."

It was 12:20 A.M. Wednesday morning, July 22, 1953.

I went up and shook hands with Mr. Velde. Numerous friends crowded about. They had remained in the hearing room until after midnight. I had promised to give a press interview and felt obligated to do so. It was unnecessary. The men had the facts. They, too, were weary. One or two questions were asked. "Did you think you were treated fairly?" I said, "It is an extremely difficult question to answer. I think I was treated personally with reasonable respect, but the procedure, however, is one I think that could destroy the reputation of any individual."

A Methodist minister drove us home. It was not far. The courtesy touched me deeply. I found it impossible to sleep. It was quiet out of doors at two that morning. There was tumult within my heart. It seemed incredible to me that a man who had sought to serve his country in an honored profession had gone through such an experience. I knew my friends of press and radio had appraised the situation with uncanny accuracy. "They" had been out to get me. I did not know at that moment whether they had been successful or not. It would depend upon the press, the radio and television. If there were a fair reporting of fact and an appraisal of motive that reflected my spirit, I thought the day might prove justified. I knew there had been an attempt to portray me as an unthinking "dupe." I knew the introduction of one exhibit after another was designed to carry the impression of a subversive, cornered at last. I realized there was no intention to face the facts of a vicious and un-American procedure, no willingness, in fact, to change a false record. I had seen the controlling members of the Committee marshaling every resource available to defend the Committee. I knew they were not politically astute. Abler men would have seen the wisdom of treating a bishop with respect, and of opening the hearing with a courteous request, "Bishop, you have requested the privilege of appearing before this Committee. We are eager to hear what you have to say. After you have presented such matters as you believe to be pertinent, it may be we will wish to ask questions." If I had failed to present convincing material, the Committee could then, quite properly, have made its queries, but if I had been able to show the files were inaccurate and that the practice of releasing them was harmful, the Committee chairman could have thanked me for the presentation, could have assured me that corrections would be made, and that harmful practices would be eliminated. I had really thought some political wisdom might have been manifest that day.

But I now knew that Mr. Jackson would continue to write in his letters, "The detailed documentation is very voluminous and would be much too lengthy to include in a letter of this kind"; that Mr. Clardy would continue to write Methodist ministers, "The facts, as related by the bishop, are in almost every case wholly without foundation. . . . The Committee did not go after the Bishop or make any charges against him, as you seem to think. It did not 'release' anything about him. . . . I challenge the Bishop to cite a single file he has inspected. Knowing that he has never seen one (other than the fragmentary material he obtained through the collaboration of a newspaper and concerning himself only), and knowing also that the wild generalization about all the files is based upon that one supposed instance, I am inclined to doubt the good faith of the Bishop." His most astounding statement was "the public would have had no knowledge of those things except for the action of the Bishop." In one breath we are told the Committee puts a disclaimer at the beginning of every file released indicating that it does not vouch for the accuracy of the material, and in Mr. Clardy's letters, we are told the material was not given out to the public, and that the public would have had no knowledge of things except for the actions of the Bishop. Mr. Clardy had read the release. He knew the Committee was releasing such material. What does one make of this kind of statement?

As I sat in the living room that night, unable to sleep, I thought back through the years, and tried to find explanation of these attacks.

I had returned to Los Angeles from the theological seminary in the early summer of 1916. After two months of preaching in the First Methodist Church at Phoenix while the pastor was on vacation, I attended the Southern California Conference which met at Santa Ana. I was appointed to a little rural charge in the San Joaquin valley at a place called Poplar. It was something of a disappointment, because I had prepared to serve upon the East Side of the city of Los Angeles. I had dreamed of bringing the religion of Jesus to the labor movement of that great city and of demonstrating that religion in service to the foreign-born and the dispossessed.

Within thirty days after reaching Poplar, I received a letter from the District Superintendent of the Los Angeles District, Dr. E. P. Ryland, stating that the Los Angeles Missionary and Church Extension Society with the concurrence of the Bishop wanted me to come at once to Los Angeles and to take up work on the East Side. It was like an answer to prayer, but the dear people at Poplar had already voted to tear down the old church building and to construct a parsonage. They had agreed to build a new church. It seemed unfair to leave. I wrote Dr. Ryland to this effect and he agreed to wait until the following October. The parsonage and the church were built. It was hard to leave the friends in this lovely rural community, but the call to the city could not be denied.

The fact that the Los Angeles building was in disrepair and had a debt of fifteen thousand dollars upon it, that there was no congregation and little financial support, did not impress us. This was the East Side. Our dream was coming true. The salary seemed munificent. I had been receiving six hundred dollars a year at Poplar, and this was to be eighteen hundred dollars. Of course, we had to pay our rent out of that, but the door had opened.

I seized every opportunity to speak. It never entered my mind to ask, is this a group fit to be addressed? These were individuals and I thought there was a message that I was summoned to preach. I knew something of the bitter background of the labor struggle in Los Angeles, the dynamiting of the Times Building, the so-called open shop town which was really a closed shop to union workers. I learned that there were subversive agencies, unpatriotic and un-American, with which one could not co-operate.

Before I entered college, I had graduated from the Los Angeles Business College and sought work. The opportunity came. I was offered a job as a stenographer with the Pacific Electric Railroad. The salary was fifty dollars a month and I was required to buy my own typewriter, paying five dollars a month on account. I had to sign a statement that I would not join a labor union. At that time, I did not understand the meaning of the "Yellow Dog" contract. I was supposed to have Saturday afternoons off, but had been advised that in the event there had been an accident, I might have to remain on to take testimony. That meant I worked nearly every Saturday afternoon.

In addition to the regular Sunday services, we centered on building up the institutional service of the church, the Boys' Clubs, the Girls' Clubs, the Clinic, the noon luncheon for the laundry operatives, and much more. But I had been sent there to establish relationships between the church and labor. A thoroughgoing social survey of the East Side was conducted, and I became acquainted with the conditions of work in many of the industrial establishments. The electrical contractors of the city requested me to preside at a meeting in which they themselves organized so that they might deal with organized labor. The purpose was to bargain collectively. The Social Creed of the Churches had affirmed that the churches stand "for the right of employers and employees alike to organize and to bargain collectively through representatives of their own choosing." I knew that too much of American industry had been organized upon a war basis and that stubborn leaders had squared off to slug it out. There had been a nation-wide attempt to forestall the organization of labor and the development of an espionage system. There had been much of violence, and the leadership that emerged was the leadership of war. Generals seldom make successful political leaders. I looked forward to the day when intelligent leaders of business might sit at a table with intelligent leaders of labor and think their problems out. Thus, when the contractors proposed collective bargaining, I thought we were making progress.

But one of the contractors, much troubled, came to me and said, "We cannot go through with this." I asked why. He said, "The banks have informed us that if we deal with organized labor they will call every piece of paper they hold against us." This was my first experience with a mailed fist clothed in the kid glove. It was respectable violence, but none the less effective. I conveyed this information to the leader of the electrical workers, and said, "I think I know what your reaction will be, but believe me you can better afford to take a licking now and win public opinion than to turn to violence. If you take the long view, be patient." He said he did not think he could keep the men in line. At a matter of fact, he could not. At that time, the great Grauman Theater job was under construction. The men cut the tags off that intricate wiring, conduits were filled with concrete. The situation became violent. I had failed.

There were intimate associations with the Jewish clothing contractors and the employees who belonged to the Amalgamated Clothing Workers.

I spoke in place after place, trying to enunciate Christian ideals, trying to win friends just as a missionary does who goes overseas. I sat in the temple with the Buddhist priests when we celebrated the Twenty-five Hundredth Anniversary of the Birth of Buddha. An invitation to spend a year in the Orient offered unusual opportunities to know the background of some of the people I served. And so, on December 5, 1918, I had sailed with Dr. Sherwood Eddy and visited Japan, China and India. I had unique opportunity to study missions, social work and the labor movement in these countries. Upon my return, I was overwhelmed by invitations to discuss the Orient.

One invitation was to address a meeting at Music Arts Hall. I had understood it to be under proper auspices, but when I reached the Hall, I noted a handbill which indicated that the meeting was under the auspices of Kuo Min Tang-Chinese Party, The Workers-Communist Party, and the Japanese Workers' Association, and that the net proceeds of collections were to go to Chinese strikers. Mrs. Oxnam had accompanied me to the meeting. I turned to her there in the foyer and said that I did not think I ought to speak at such a meeting and that I had been misinformed concerning its sponsors. I did not speak. I was astounded to find that *The Daily Worker* took cognizance of an obscure young preacher and ran an excoriating article entitled, "Pulpit Pounder Fails to Speak."

Subsequently, railway workers went out on strike. Maintenance-of-way men had been receiving but sixty dollars a month, working out of doors at all seasons. Railroad leadership should have been far in advance of such conditions and should have instituted changes long before the strike occurred. Sound collective bargaining would have avoided such a disturbance. Strikers were denied a place to meet and were subject to federal injunctions that well nigh tied their hands. I told the men they might meet in the auditorium of our church. The leader of this strike later became a Methodist preacher. Many of the men joined the church, but I was getting my eye teeth cut.

I soon learned that there were men "uptown" who were opposed to a young minister dabbling in matters that were none of his business. One Labor Day, I addressed a great audience out of doors at Brookfield Park in Pasadena and spoke upon the theme, "Some Lessons Labor Needs to Learn." I did not know that William Bennet Munro, an authority upon municipal administration and political science, professor of Harvard University, was present. He sent me a copy of his next volume on citizenship and indicated the page upon which he had included the essential points of that address. It had been a plea for the recognition of spiritual values. I had stressed the fact that labor needs a unifying force other than an enemy.

It was at this moment that a vacancy occurred upon the Board of Education. One of its members had been appointed a judge. I was quite taken off my feet when I learned that I was to be nominated to succeed this gentleman. I thought it a public service and gave consent. But the forces "uptown" thought it unwise, and when the vote was taken three voted for me and three for another. Thus no one was elected, and within a short time, city elections were to be held when such matters would be settled by the populace as a whole. I received a petition signed by the high school teachers of the city, requesting me to stand for election to the Board of Education. A great bond issue had been authorized, and the teachers felt there were some who were more interested in building contracts and insurance premiums than they were in the children. They wanted someone on the Board who would represent what they believed to be the interest of the student. I was very young. I little realized what a political campaign would be. In the primary elections, I was nominated. Then the full force of reaction was loosed. The Los Angeles *Times* carried a headline to the effect that there was an astounding scheme abroad "to sovietize the public schools." This story grew out of the fact that I had answered a question in a forum. Somone had asked, "Do you favor getting the opinions of the teaching staff of the city when policy is being formed?" I said that I did and that some way ought to be developed whereby the thinking of the teachers themselves could be made available to the Board when decisions of policy were taken.

I had the support of the teachers, the ministers, of labor, and support from influential men of business and women who were leading the Women's Clubs. It was in the midst of the campaign that a strike broke out at San Pedro. I was familiar with some of the conditions under which seamen worked. The so-called hiring halls were close to slave markets. Racketeers were in the picture. It was an explosive situation.

The IWW had called the strike, and no doubt was prepared to resort to the tactics of war. They held that there was nothing in common between employer and employee. The IWW was a revolutionary force, and its practice of sabotage had done much damage in the lumber camps and in areas where casual workers had harvested the crops. Instead of studying the brilliant researches of Carleton Parker and of facing the issue in terms of removing the causes that produce such philosophy, reactionary employers responded in kind. Violence was met by violence. Criminal syndicalist laws had been passed. Former criminals had been used as professional witnesses, and labor leaders had been railroaded into prison. It was felt the way to deal with such matters was to resort to force repression.

All of this was present in the San Pedro strike. The Los Angeles Police Department was commandeered. Several hundred workers were arrested without warrant. They were held long enough to break the strike. Some testified later that they were beaten by policemen. I heard the testimony of some of them. The Chief of Police who engineered that strike-breaking job was subsequently dismissed for conduct unbecoming an officer and for liquor addiction. Upton Sinclair, the novelist and socialist, went to San Pedro and held a protest meeting. He tried to read the Declaration of Independence and was arrested. I was appalled. This, to me, was in keeping with the methods of Russia. It was un-American. There was a better way to handle such matters. Mr. Sinclair advised me that he was going to rent the Walker Auditorium and to hold a protest meeting. I knew that if I attended such a meeting, I would never be elected to the Board of Education. I knew it would be misinterpreted. I weighed the matter carefully. It seemed to me then as a young man that election to the Board of Education was less important than standing for the Bill of Rights. I knew that if our civil liberties were abrogated, there would be no way to settle the industrial struggle peacefully. It may have been a mistake. Perhaps it was. I did go to the meeting and offered prayer.

In the prayer, I had said, "Give to us, we pray, the spirit of tolerance. . . . But as we pray for tolerance, we pray, too, that we may be men of conviction. Give to us an open mind, but give to us also the strength to stand for our convictions even if it take a Calvary Cross to win them. May we never bow the knee before insolent might. Help us to be tender and just, loving and righteous, never turning aside from the needy. Give to us that virtue that was Christ's —forgiveness. May we even love those who despitefully use us. Keep before us ever the example of the One who was despised and rejected of men, yet who could pray for forgiveness of those who crucified Him."

It was, of course, the prayer of a young man and its weaknesses are quickly discernible, but its closing paragraph rang true. "We thank Thee for America, her traditions, her history, her place in the world. We thank Thee for our forefathers who won for us the

liberties we so easily inherit. Give to us their spirit. . . . We thank
Thee for the Constitution of our Republic. We thank Thee that
the people united to establish justice, to insure domestic tranquillity,
and promote the general welfare. . . . Give to us the courage today
to stand as Americans insisting upon the maintenance of those
principles upon which our Republic was founded."

Some statements were made from that platform that evening that
I thought to be unfortunate and unwise, but generally speakers held
to the essential purpose of the meeting which was to protest the
abrogation of civil liberties upon the part of those charged with
enforcing the law.

It was true. The next morning the headlines screamed. I, of course,
was beaten in the election.

But I foolishly thought, that was that. I was soon to learn otherwise.

There were agencies then, as now, that can be used to defame.
One was called the Better America Federation, and before many
months had passed, its executive had filed charges against me as a
Methodist minister. In his letter to the Bishop, he said, "It is with the
greatest sorrow that I have compiled the data concerning this pastor
of our denomination." Strangely enough, the charges which he filed
in 1923 were the items upon which Mr. Kunzig was to question
me in 1953. He referred to the meeting I had never addressed. He
alleged that I "was advertised to speak and did speak" at a meeting
that I had never addressed. He used the very words that Mr. Kunzig
used in describing that meeting.

One of the specifications stated, "One of Mr. Oxnam's trusted
lieutenants, an enthusiastic teacher in his Sunday School, has been
Mrs. Kaschub." He said that she had been teaching the children
from nine to eleven years of age and had used Walter Thomas Mills'
book entitled *The Struggle for Existence* as a textbook. He alleged this book "is wonderfully adapted to make it easy to understand socialism, not only for the children, but also for the grown

ups." This was so absurd upon its face as to be laughable, if it were not so vicious. But he climaxed it by saying, "On a certain Sunday morning, not long since, in the Sunday School Class of Mrs. Kaschub the following program was carried out. First—the studies in socialism lasted one hour. Second, there was one hour of dancing. Third, there was twenty minutes of singing—the meeting closed by singing 'The Worker's Flag is the Red Flag.' " Ministers would rejoice if they could have two hours and twenty minutes for church school. The truth was Mrs. Martha Kaschub was not a regular teacher in the church school. An affidavit signed by a Roy H. Bennett, superintendent of the church school and a businessman of Los Angeles, indicates that she taught in the church school but once as a substitute teacher on February 25. She taught a class of girls in Grade Two in the Junior Department, the ages being of ten and eleven. On that day, the lesson which she taught was the "Majesty of Jesus" based on Peter's answer to Christ's question, "But whom say ye that I am." Mr. Bennett swore "under our program schedule, the length of the lesson could not have exceeded twenty-five minutes." He concluded his affidavit by stating that "Mrs. Kaschub had not attended any sessions of the Sunday School following that single day upon which she taught and that she, therefore, was never nominated before the Board as a teacher in the above said Sunday School."

Another specification alleged "The Boy Scout movement of the Church of All Nations (Methodist Episcopal) is in charge of a young Russian, socialist, by the name of Klussman [sic]." But Wes H. Klusmann, who is today one of the chief executives of the Boy Scouts of America, in a sworn affidavit said that he was born in the city of Los Angeles in 1897, that his parents were American citizens, and that they never resided outside the state of California, "that affiant is not a socialist, has never been registered as a socialist, nor has he ever studied the doctrines of socialism nor attempted to teach them." He went on to say that "to his knowledge, he has no Russian ancestry." He was in charge of the boys' work program at the Church of All Nations and swore, "The Boy Scout program was carried out according to the policies prescribed by the National Council of the Boy Scouts of America, and said institution was in thorough accord and sympathy with the Boy Scout movement."

A third, and the last that I shall set forth, was that the Library of the Church of All Nations was "in charge of Alberta Martin." He alleged that Alberta Martin "taught children at the Socialist Lyceum in the days of Job Harriman. Alberta Martin's chief ambition in life is to make socialists out of young people and children. That is how she became radical, according to her story." Alberta Martin in a sworn affidavit stated that "she had worked at the Church of all Nations in the year 1920 when she was fifteen years of age, that to her knowledge, she had never seen Job Harriman nor was she at all familiar with his work, that she never taught children at the Socialist Lyceum, nor was she familiar with the fact, nor does she now know, that such a school or institution was in existence." It so happens that Alberta Martin was five years of age at the time Job Harriman was prominent in the political life of Los Angeles.

A reasonable man can scarce credit such actions. The Southern California Annual Conference through its duly constituted committee, after examining the charges and checking the facts, reported that they were groundless and dismissed the entire matter. The Annual Conference was so incensed that it elected me a delegate to the General Conference, an honor seldom coming to a young man of thirty-three years of age.

As I sat there that evening, remembering all this, I recalled that Mrs. Elizabeth Dilling had picked up these falsehoods and had published them in *The Red Network*; that they had appeared again and again in publications of private agencies that make their living by keeping otherwise intelligent people so alarmed that they act unintelligently.

When I was elected a professor in Boston University, and subsequently was elected president of DePauw University, this material was sent to all the members of the Board of Trustees by this man who called himself a patriot, and who worked for an agency known as the Better America Federation. I had always believed that a minister should not become involved in law suits, but this had gone too far. I finally decided to sue Colonel Smith, the Better America Federation, and its responsible Board members. It seemed to me fair as a Christian minister to write E. P. Clark, the president of that organization, a wealthy and respected leader of business in Los Angeles, and set the matter before him. I was of the opinion that if I could get a retraction, that would be satisfactory. Mr. Clark responded at once and stated that he would be glad to see me and to rectify the matter if I had been wronged. I went to Los Angeles. He had Colonel Leroy F. Smith, the executive of the Better America Federation (he always put the Colonel before his name though he was but a reserve officer) come to his office. I presented the facts. They were convincing to Mr. Clark who told Colonel Smith that he must make this matter right. Colonel Smith agreed that he would make proper retraction. I agreed that I would send a full statement of the facts which were to be published in the bulletin of the Better America Federation.

I returned to the University. I was under very heavy schedule, and Mrs. Oxnam became seriously ill. It was some time before I could send the material to Colonel Smith. He wrote me twice requesting it. At the very time I forwarded the material to him, Mr. Clark died. Colonel Smith then refused to carry out his promise and issued a bulletin that repeated the libel. It was then necessary to sue him. I was preparing the case when news of Colonel Smith's death came. There was nothing further apparently that could be done, but it is this material going back through all these years that occasioned a continuing attack that seems never to end. Because I have been prominent in the Federal Council of the Churches of Christ in America and am now one of the presidents of the World Council of Churches, the attacks upon these great agencies have centered upon the leaders, and I, being among them, have been named again and again.

I wondered, as I sat there thinking of the day, whether this could ever be brought to an end, and I reached the conclusion that whether it were a continuing fight or whether this hearing would end it, there was nothing to do but to maintain a spirit of good will, to move forward with determination, and to keep the light of publicity upon those practices that do endanger freedom.

I was utterly unprepared for the response of the American press. The great papers of the nation carried banner headlines. More than 80 per cent of the editorials were favorable, some of them extravagantly generous. *The New York Times* gave front-page coverage and published my statement in full. The National Broadcasting Company televised thirty minutes of the hearing and had done a piece of selection that commends itself to all who were present.

Some friends were generous enough to say that the hearing will mark a turn in our national life and that the un-American practices of some of these investigators will be brought to an end. I think they overestimate the significance of that day. But the fact that men are speaking out everywhere, that strong statements have been issued by the Presbyterian Church and by the bishops of the Protestant Episcopal Church as well as the Council of Bishops of the Methodist Church, all indicate a trend, and if it be that the protest of one has been helpful in eliciting the protest of the many, and that out of protest may come constructive suggestions for reform, then the day was well spent.

Set in Intertype Garamond
Format by Katharine Sitterly
Manufactured by The Haddon Craftsmen, Inc.
Published by Harper & Brothers, *New York*